A BETTER WAY TO BUDGET

A BETTER WAY TO BUDGET

BUILDING SUPPORT FOR BOLD, **STUDENT-CENTERED** CHANGE IN PUBLIC SCHOOLS

NATHAN LEVENSON

Harvard Education Press
Cambridge, Massachusetts

Library of Congress Control Number 2015938617

Paperback 978-1-61250-861-0
Library Edition ISBN 978-1-61250-862-7

Published by Harvard Education Press,
an imprint of the Harvard Education Publishing Group

Harvard Education Press
8 Story Street
Cambridge, MA 02138

Cover Design: Ciano Design
Cover Image: Creative-idea/Digital Vision Vectors/Getty Images
The typefaces used in this book are ITC Stone Sans, Knockout,
Legacy Serif ITC, and Solano Gothic

CONTENTS

WHY DO WE FIGHT OVER BUDGETS?

I have never met a superintendent, school board member, administrator, teacher, or taxpayer who didn't want to help children be successful in life. In a highly polarized country, we all actually agree that a solid education is critical to our children and our collective future. Why, then, do school budgets become a bruising battleground? So fierce are these battles that it is common for district leaders to propose budgets that don't reflect what they think is best for their students. Why do school boards pass these less-than-best budgets and, worse, why do so many leaders who push hard for ensuring every precious dollar is doing the most good for students lose their job or their political capital?

I remember the advice I received just before starting as superintendent in Arlington, Massachusetts. Like so many other new district leaders, I made the trek to visit a revered sage, a former uber-successful superintendent who seemed to have all the answers. As I eagerly outlined my goals and plans, he held up his hand to stop me and said, "Nate, no superintendent ever got fired because the kids can't read. They get fired for how they tried to help kids to read." I dismissed this advice as the cynicism that comes with age, politely cut the meeting short, and wondered how he ever got to be so respected.

With the arrogance and energy that come from the dangerous mix of naïveté and passion, supercharged by a near-twenty-year career in the private sector, I set out to make sure every student in my district could read and master higher-order thinking skills, and so much more. The facts that the district had only a moderate level of spending, near the state average, and that revenue was shrinking even as enrollment and costs were growing didn't dent my determination. I knew how to manage finances, and with expert guidance from a very wise cabinet and team of principals, quickly mapped a plan to accomplish our ambitious goals for our students.

Then everything hit the fan. My cabinet had assumed I would be asking (begging and pleading, actually) the town for more money to implement our improvement agenda. I had no expectations that more money was coming, so I had always intended to spend the dollars we did have differently—to fund our priorities and cut elsewhere. A few days after presenting my budget, just after dozens of administrators, many board members, and a multitude of staff voiced wild opposition to the budget, I again made the trek to visit the sage former superintendent. I listened more closely this time.

This book is the product of many years of collecting such advice from many wise and successful district leaders, coupled with the experience I've gained as a partner at the District Management Council—a firm that works with school districts across the country, helping them raise achievement despite tight resources—and my personal experience as a superintendent and school board leader. It is also the product of my experience working across the country with K–12 district leaders to implement a set of ideas for doing more with less, which I collected in a 2012 book called *Smarter Budgets, Smarter Schools* (Harvard Education Press). While there has been strong acceptance by leaders to many of the ideas in that book (even those I called "crazy"), I have realized that sharing these ideas for resource reallocation was not enough. One of the most common questions I receive now as a consultant is: How do I get the school board, principals, central office, town/city, and other stakeholders to support rather than fight these changes? This new book is written to provide strategies and guidance to school superintendents, central office leaders, building principals, and school board members interested in learning how to improve the budgeting process so that bold, student-centered ideas can be passed. It will focus on improving the *process of budgeting* in order to avoid or overcome political push-back and technical barriers that typically stymie attempts to boldly shift resources. While building off the previous book, this book is written so that no prior knowledge is needed and is intended as a stand-alone resource to help educators implement any bold decisions, including but not limited to the ideas in *Smarter Budgets, Smarter Schools.*

It has been my mission to learn how to peacefully build great budgets and shift funds to help students. I have learned much and discerned eight lessons worth sharing in the following chapters about how to build and maintain support for bold, student-centered budgets—what I refer to as "smarter budgets" in this book—especially when tough choices and some pain are part of the plan. In the process I have become optimistic that the needs of students, staff, and taxpayers can be balanced in a way that will prepare all students for a productive and fulfilling future.

While many districts struggle to build a balanced budget given the growing needs of students and limited resources, passing a balanced budget is an absolute must, and more than 99 percent of school districts do it every year. They make tough decisions, add programs, cut staff or pay, and balance their budget. It's seldom fun, but always done, and usually on time and accurately—that is to say, when the year ends, expenses do typically match revenue.

So why does anyone need a book on passing smarter budgets, if nearly every district already can build, pass, and deliver a balanced budget no matter how deep the cuts? Because far too many districts aren't passing the *best* budgets, just balanced ones. They are making the wrong cuts, postponing needed investments, and, paradoxically, sometimes not cutting enough in order to improve outcomes! The vast majority of district leaders I meet have good ideas for how to raise achievement or expand the arts or support the social and emotional needs of children with the dollars they have, but they can't garner the support for all of these changes. They can't pass a budget that does the most good for the most children.

Historically, many school districts have equated improvement efforts with new funding. If lots of kids struggle to read, then hiring reading teachers or buying READ 180 software seems a logical step to remedy the situation. Of course, this requires extra dollars for salary, technology, and training. If too many students are dropping out, then hiring more counselors might be the answer. Too often, these thoughtful and reasonable responses are predicated on a big grant, a local tax increase, or more state aid. They all start with new dollars.

The modern history of K–12 education has been a steady, significant increase in real, inflation-adjusted, per-pupil spending. It has increased steadily for over fifty years. The recent financial crisis and competing demands for municipal, state, and federal dollars have changed all this. Spending is down and likely to be very tight for years to come (see figure I.1).

This constant growth in spending has created in many districts a Pavlovian response in which they solve challenges with new programs that require new funds. In a world without growing budgets, will new programs be started? Will challenges go unaddressed?

The optimistic view is that even as budgets tighten, new challenges will be forcefully addressed because old programs will be cut so new ones can be started. Often called "addition by subtraction," it's a commonsense response to growing needs and shrinking revenue—but it's a difficult one. Its cousin strategy, "pruning the garden," which calls for ending less effective, strategically less important efforts to preserve more important

FIGURE I.1
Inflation-adjusted per-pupil spending

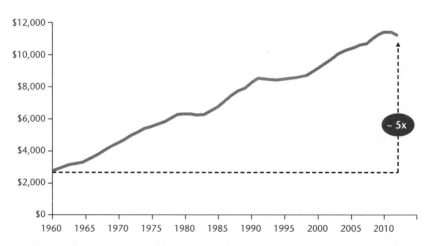

Source: Adapted from US Department of Education, National Center for Education Statistics, "Mobile Digest of Education Statistics 2013," http://nces.ed.gov/programs/digest/mobile/. Shows current dollars (not including capital outlays and interest on debt).

ones, is another thoughtful response to tight budgets. In the best of worlds, district budgets will fund strategic priorities, shift resources as student needs shift, and abandon programs that aren't effective or cost-effective.

Unfortunately, the most common response to tight budgets is a nasty, difficult battle over what stays and what is trimmed. What would help the most children is just one of many considerations, and often not the deciding factor.

Every superintendent, school board member, central office administrator, principal, education reformer, and all their friends and loved ones know that passing a district budget that includes big changes, even if the changes are just great for kids, is hard—very hard, in fact. Packed school board meetings, tears, anger, mean letters to the editor, and fierce pushback often leave thoughtful, good-for-kids budgets stripped of much of what was wanted, and the status quo or across-the-board reductions are passed in its place.

Nearly all school and district leaders can share a story or two about how hard it was to make bold, sweeping changes to school budgets. These stories often include imagery of intense conflict, such as "budget battles," "brutal fights," or "a grinding assault." The conflict is framed as a battle—between reform and status quo, or kids and adults, or two other such "opponents."

A more nuanced and more helpful way to understand (and thus effectively manage) the seemingly ever-present conflicts during budget season is to see the struggle as a tug-of-war between two equally noble and reasonable sets of values: valuing organizational health and valuing higher student achievement. Both are important, but sometimes they are at odds (see figure I.2).

FIGURE I.2
Values tug-of-war

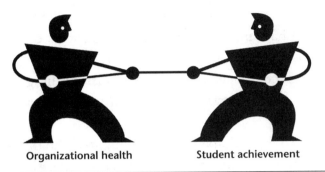

| Organizational health | Student achievement |

Image courtesy of Microsoft clip art/Creative Commons

Organizational health means having pride in the school or district, wanting people to feel valued, caring about the feelings of others, and ensuring financial stability for hardworking, dedicated staff. These values seem like a moral compass pointing toward true north. Don't we all want to feel pride in our schools or care about caring people? Would we want to work with others who didn't have these values? Would we want to lead an organization that didn't care about these goals, or want a leader who didn't embrace these values?

All the district leaders I know value a caring organization, and all the educators I have met want students to achieve at high levels. We all care about the health of our organization (its people) and raising student achievement. Unfortunately, declining budgets cause a tug-of-war between these sometimes-competing values that reside in us all.

Organizations also have collective experiences that shape their belief systems. Often, and with good cause, these past experiences can lead to limited support for new reforms embodied in student-centric budgets. It's not that people don't want to help more kids learn more, it's that they don't really believe a given reform will likely help many students.

Atticus Finch, the wise country lawyer from *To Kill a Mockingbird,* would have made a great superintendent and likely been able to pass bold, smart budgets because he knew "you never really understand a person until you consider things from his point of view . . . until you climb into his skin and walk around in it."

In the next eight chapters we are going to climb into the skin of those who most often come to school board meetings to fight next year's budget, who write letters, send e-mails, call hundreds to fight against the proposed budget, and generally make passing smarter budgets so damn hard. The goal is not to demean them, but to understand their legitimate concerns and craft specific, concrete strategies for winning them over, minimizing any pain, and diminishing the number who follow their lead.

Fully understanding why good people, who place a high premium on organizational health, fight changes to how limited dollars might be spent will provide a road map for shaping and managing future budgets in a way that is more likely to produce a result that's good for kids and better for the organization, without draining all the political capital of school and district leaders.

These are eight lessons that can help ensure every district budget is doing the most good for the most children while respecting the real needs of teachers, administrators, and other stakeholders.

MAKE CHANGE FEEL NORMAL

It's just human nature: most people don't like change. We grow comfortable with what we know, have figured out how to manage and navigate the current system, often grow to like the status quo, and often worry that the new will be worse. Companies that made desktop computers didn't want to make laptops, and many laptop makers had no use for tablets. Even without the pressure of new technology, Sears didn't want to act like Target or Walmart, even as its customers left in droves to those other retailers.

While we can't rewire the human psyche, some districts have created systems, procedures, and eventually cultures that are more open to change and thus more easily embrace big shifts in spending more easily.

BUILD A VISION BEFORE BUILDING A BUDGET

Outwardly, most budget battles center on what's funded and what's not. Just below the surface, however, the battle is really about differing visions of what's needed, what's good for kids, even what's possible. By first surfacing these differing visions, and by investing time to forge a shared vision for the future, we can eliminate one major contributor to budget-induced conflict.

ENGAGE AND ENLIST PRINCIPALS

It is easy to rustle up people who will oppose a tough budget decision, but fortunately—with some planning and time—district leaders can also proactively increase the number of people who will strongly support important but hard changes in spending. A linchpin to building broad, active support for these types of changes is meaningful engagement and leadership of school principals, who have a unique and influential role with parents and staff alike.

TAKE STEPS TO MINIMIZE THE PAIN

With tight or declining resources, most new initiatives will require some people losing their jobs, being transferred to roles or schools not of their choosing, or adopting practices not of their choice. This hurts, and good people rightfully resist hurting their colleagues, friends, or teachers of their children. It would be overpromising to suggest that bold, student-centered budgets can be achieved without any pain, but a number of strategies can reduce the sting, minimize the negative impact, and thus build sufficient support to allocate resources in ways that are best for students and fair to staff.

WIN OVER SUPPORTERS THROUGH JOINT FACT FINDING

A surprisingly large amount of the disagreement on spending decisions stems from a surprisingly large disagreement on the facts of the current situation. There is almost no end to the degree to which smart people bring different facts to the discussion—from the financial health of the district to the number of struggling students, the effectiveness of a given program, or even what is legal in the state. If people can't agree on the facts, they are very unlikely to agree on what constitutes a smart use of funds. Extensive research has shown that a formal process of joint fact finding can bring common understanding and widespread support for change.

MAKE BOLD AND COMPREHENSIVE PLANS

Perhaps the best news of all is that the better the plan, the easier it is to build support for hard budget decisions. Conversely, if compromise means undermining a new effort's effectiveness, it will also undermine support. Some simple rules can offer guidance on when to compromise and when to hold firm.

CRAFT MESSAGES THAT RESONATE WITH STAKEHOLDERS

District budgets are complex, efforts to raise achievement are nuanced, and trade-offs are not easily understood by staff and the public. It's hard to talk about school spending in a way that is clear and compelling, but it's critically important. Some district leaders have developed much finesse and can craft persuasive messages that are easily understood and compelling, which expands the number of supporters and reduces pushback.

GET THE MESSAGE OUT TO ALL SUPPORTERS AND POTENTIAL SUPPORTERS

Getting the word out is hard and misinformation can spread like wildfire. Traditional methods of communicating, like budget forums and school committee presentations, aren't doing the job in many districts. New technologies, influence mapping, and lessons from Madison Avenue can be adapted to K–12 to make communications more impactful and counterbalance the roar of opponents.

Taken together, these eight lessons can help districts build budgets that increase student learning, balance the needs of others, and, most importantly, get passed with less angst and anger. Collectively, they are reason to be optimistic that tight resources needn't stymie efforts to help more kids achieve in more ways.

1

MAKE CHANGE FEEL NORMAL

*Apply Strategies to Make Changes to Spending Less
Controversial and More Easily Accepted*

When I saw on the nightly news the fall of the Berlin
Wall, I commented to a friend, "The world changed today." What I meant by this was that something rare and important had happened. Something that would have lasting,
widespread impact—the end of the Cold War, peace between
nuclear powers, and much relief for the federal budget, as mil-
itary spending would be scaled back. Sure, I turned out to be
wrong in many ways, but it felt like something monumental
had just happened.

The next time I heard this phrase uttered, with the same
wondrous appreciation of the moment in time, was when a
principal heard that I wanted to change how we served students participating in an integration program. For the principal, the announcement was full of shock and awe. For me, it
was unexciting, obvious, and bordering on the mundane.

The facts, as I knew them, were easy to understand.

We served one hundred students from a nearby city, who
started in kindergarten and stayed in the district through

graduation. The district had been busing in students voluntarily for nearly forty years and the students fared terribly:

- Upward of 50 percent were placed on IEPs (individual-
  ized education programs).
- Very few went to college, despite the fact that nearly
  95 percent of their classmates did.
- Even though they had attended district schools since
  kindergarten, more than half failed multiple courses in
  high school.
- Climate surveys indicated that most of the students felt
  unwelcome and unwanted.

I certainly expected—welcomed, actually—an energetic back
and forth about *what* to change, and *how* to change, but never
anticipated resistance as to *whether* to change a program that
so underserved one hundred of our students.

The district leadership team spent months debating if the
program should remain as is. Oddly, no one disputed the hor-
rific outcomes or doubted the lost opportunity to help one
hundred students who rode a bus for more than an hour each
day for thirteen years. Everything centered on whether we
could change a program that had been in place, unaltered, for
so long. I dismissed this concern as a mix of cowardice over ad-
dressing an issue involving race, face saving by not admitting
we had failed many children for decades, and a general comfort
with the status quo.

Hardly for the first time, and certainly not for the last, my
cabinet was wiser than I was. I pushed forward because the facts
demanded we change. We would shift extra help services from
paraprofessionals to teachers; add a late bus so the students
could more easily participate in after-school programs, athlet-

ics, and clubs; and bring in expert college counselors to shepherd students through the application, selection, and financial aid processes. To pay for this, we would reduce the number of administrators overseeing the program and shift money currently dedicated to professional development conference fees.

I was completely unprepared for what happened next. The day I announced the plan, a Fox News TV crew showed up at my house, hundreds of angry parents and teachers came to the school board meeting, and the press called consistently. Long before I finished sharing the stats, and before the plan was fully outlined to the public, a supporter on the school board kindly suggested that the district wasn't ready for changing this program. So we didn't.

I learned three lessons from this disappointing situation:

1. Always call your wife to warn her that a Fox News crew will be knocking at the door.
2. Don't dismiss the anxiety of principals.
3. The less things change, the harder it is to change things.

As we conducted a postmortem on our failed attempt to help these one hundred students in need, we realized two things about our district. Staffing seldom changed unless forced by budget cuts, and programs were seldom formally reviewed for effectiveness. This had created a culture—shared by parents, administrators, and teachers alike—that placed a high value on stability.

In education we talk about change a lot. Pick your favorite saying:

- "The more things change, the more they stay the same."
- "They keep moving my cheese."

- "This too shall pass."
- "The only constant is change."
- "The definition of insanity is doing the same thing over and over, but expecting different results."

We have too much change, we need more, or with a sigh and a shrug we acknowledge that we seem to be on a merry-go-round that won't stop. Change is thrown at us from many directions, including new state regulations like teacher evaluation and Common Core, new federal programs driven by the No Child Left Behind Act of 2001 (NCLB) or NCLB waivers, grant requirements, the latest collective bargaining compromises, shifting priorities from an ever-changing school board, or morphing student demographics. Outside pressures force change on school districts. In many districts, the budget is a counterbalancing force. Developed in large part by district leaders, it can be a tool to provide stability to a workforce that works hard and is tossed around by external pressures.

Every caring organization should value providing stability and peace of mind for its staff, especially when the state, the federal government, and others seem to keep shifting the ground underneath them. While district budget builders can't set how much money the district will spend, they recommend to the school board how to spend what dollars they have. In good times this often meant adding new programs to address student needs, in many cases layering them on top of the existing programs. Seemingly, children got what was needed and adults achieved stability. It felt like a win-win.

In the current era of tight budgets, some yearn for those good old days. When we look back on them, however, we see that this "add through layering" approach might not have been the best strategy for raising achievement. The very reason a new program was needed may have been that the old one wasn't working. Holding on to the past commits some students to ineffective efforts. Also, in a relatively short school day, every minute counts, and keeping past efforts further splinters a student's time.

I've seen firsthand how preserving the past can ease the way for the new but be detrimental to students. After an honest assessment of its reading intervention programs, a district concluded it had failed far too many students. About a third of the kids in its suburban elementary schools read below grade level, and 90 percent of struggling readers failed to make a year's progress each year. They fell further behind when receiving intervention services. The district was trying hard and had four large-scale reading intervention efforts under way, each staffed by a different funding source. Opting to implement a general education–led intervention effort, district leaders decided that since they could afford the new and keep the old, they would. It seemed to them very unfair to eliminate the existing reading staff or bump them into new schools or roles. It would be better for all if they stayed put, the district figured. Then the unintended consequences started. In some schools students with IEPs were denied the new reading services, because there wouldn't be enough work for all the special educators. In other schools children of poverty didn't get the more effective interventions because Title I staff needed full schedules. Perhaps the oddest compromise was to provide some students both Title I reading and gen ed intervention (using different and conflicting materials), but this required pulling these struggling students from math three times a week, adding numeracy to their list of struggles.

As budgets have gotten tight, the layering approach is much less of an option, but it has often been replaced with another stability-enhancing strategy: across-the-board cuts. Part of the appeal of such cuts is that they make a small impact across a wide swath of the district. The change in any one school or department or program is small. It's a way to minimize the amount of change and provide as much stability as possible given reduced funding. Unfortunately, the best use of limited dollars demands much more fluid use of funds. As enrollment shifts, as programs are evaluated, and as new needs emerge, dollars should be spent differently in response. The trick is to find ways to shift funds more often, while still providing peace of mind and a sense of stability to the organization. Fortunately, some savvy superintendents have done just this. They have systematically created cultures that accept more change without staff, parents, and the community feeling overwhelmed or attacked.

For more than fifteen years I have sought out superintendents and school districts that seemed to implement frequent, bold improvements to serving their students without raising staff anxiety and generating frenzied pushback. My conversations with these lucky or skillful superintendents, searching for their secrets, have often ended on an unsatisfying note. "It wasn't all that special. It needed to be done and it's just what we do in this district," they say. I doubt that something in the drinking water made their parents and community members more passive than others, that the school lunches made staff more agreeable than most, or that contract provisions made their principals less protective of their staff than others, but these districts have had an easier time winning support for big, bold, student-centered shifts in spending, despite all the usual pain and suffering it has caused some staff, departments, or programs.

At first I credited this to the skill of the (humble and modest) superintendents: they must be politically astute coalition builders who know how to win friends and influence strangers. When I realized that these districts had a long history of such budget flexibility, stretching well before the current superintendent, I had to ditch this theory. Eventually I did figure out why these districts (some big, others small; urban, suburban; affluent or not) seemed to have more budget flexibility: their policies, procedures, and practices embedded flexible spending in almost everything they did. Maybe it wasn't in the water or school lunches, but it was in the air and their DNA. I learned a valuable lesson and a disappointing truth: First, districts that shift funds with relative ease have normalized change in staffing levels and patterns through the use of staffing guidelines tied to enrollment and student needs. Second, most districts really don't know what reasonable staffing levels are for many positions or what programs really help students. Professional judgment and historical staffing—rather than hard facts—guide many staffing decisions, which makes it easy for caring people to push back when changes to staffing are suggested for next year's budget.

When I visited and interviewed leaders of districts that seemed to regularly shift staff, dollars, and programs each year; more easily cut programs no longer needed; and generally had smart, flexible budgets without overwhelming or angering most of the staff, I realized that over time they had created a virtuous cycle. Because they made changes on a regular basis, change didn't seem riot-worthy—it seemed natural. These weren't districts filled with adrenaline junkies who got a thrill from change. They were regular people who would have preferred more stability, but they just didn't *expect* it.

The more flexible districts that had normalized change had clear enrollment- and need-driven guidelines for staffing, such as special education teachers provide twenty-five hours of instruction a week, art teachers teach twenty-eight classes a week, or English language learner (ELL) teachers support thirty students. These staffing guidelines were student centered, not school building centered. As a result, these teachers often worked in more than one school, and didn't balk when school assignments changed as enrollment and student needs shifted. If a school that had twenty-eight periods of art one year (a full teaching load) dropped to twenty-four, the teacher (and principal) just knew—no fight—that next year's assignment would include half a day in another school. In these districts, assignments changed each year, even during the year, as enrollment shifted.

Not so in other districts. One of the most striking examples of culturally induced inflexibility is staffing that took place in a large district facing draconian budget cuts. Faced with plunging state aid, this district with more than twenty-five thousand students had cut four hundred positions and had more cuts on the way. Benchmarking and time studies revealed that its speech and language therapy department was significantly overstaffed and its services very inefficiently delivered. Faced with this data and a multitude of other cuts looming, the district opted to reduce a handful of therapists.

No one was prepared for what ensued. With fewer therapists in the district, the remaining staff had to cover some additional schools. While the practice of working in more than one school was normal, changing schools was not. The anxiety, anger, and angst were overwhelming. Staff were infuriated that they would be dragged away from "their school" to work in "other schools." The first compromise was to reduce the cuts to speech therapists (and increase them elsewhere) and then to assign less vocal staff to more schools. Within a year, this led to bitter complaints that some therapists had much more onerous schedules and caseloads than others, so more staff should be hired back. In the end, anger and frustration permeated the department, and further changes in special education staffing were squelched, despite ample opportunities for greater efficiency and deep cuts elsewhere. The district had violated a cultural norm, and culture trumped student needs. In a district that routinely moved staff as enrollment and students shifted, this would have been a nonevent, not a ruckus.

Looking at school districts through the lens of "do we normalize change?" adds a whole new dimension to crafting policies and practices that can make shifting resources either easy, hard, or nearly impossible. This viewpoint impacts the vast majority of the budget, from teaching staff to math curriculum to dropout prevention programs and even to busing, as well as the ever-difficult class size issue.

FORMALIZE STAFFING GUIDELINES

Districts that shift funds easily generally have practices that shift staff assignments year to year in transparent, data-driven ways. They reason that it's a good way to allocate resources, but it also normalizes that things change each year in response to changing student needs. In other districts, many student-centric budget plans are dashed on the rocks of staff pushback against assignment changes. This takes many forms, such as teachers wanting to stay in the same school, grade, or courses. Attempts to free up funds are derailed when Mr. Smith leads a mini-revolt upon learning that he will be transferred from third grade to fourth, from King to Kennedy School, or from

Algebra I to tenth-grade geometry. While the small number of impacted teachers seldom stirs a public outcry, they can exert much pressure on principals and department heads who, in turn, often fail to support the overall budget plan. Some of these teachers may also have a direct line to the school board, and just a few phone calls can wilt support, especially if the callers' children were taught by Mr. Smith.

Staffing stickiness, the resistance to shifting teacher assignments, can add 3–5 percent to staffing costs, and even more in districts with declining enrollment or high student mobility. It's not uncommon for a superintendent's attempt to fill a vacant position at one school with a teacher from another school who is not actually needed (based on enrollment) to create quite a stir. Staff become very attached to their schools, which is understandable, even desirable, but also very expensive. In support services like special education, reading, ELL, or speech and language, moving staff assignments to respond to changing needs can be an act of war.

One way to normalize shifting staff in response to shifting student enrollment and needs is to formalize staffing rules. If clear, reasonable guidelines determine staffing based on student needs and enrollment, then everyone knows automatically when staff will shift, and the shifts become much less emotional.

Because these guidelines are set well in advance of knowing next year's enrollment and student needs, the impacted staff feel much less picked upon. It's not personal, because the decision to move, cut, or repurpose wasn't tied specifically to them. So often, in districts with no official or formal staffing guidelines, when they crunch the numbers and conclude that the social studies department needs one less teacher, or that a speech therapist should cover one more school, not only does the individual teacher feel targeted, but the entire school and department also feel they have been unreasonably and arbitrarily targeted. Why doesn't math lose a teacher? Why aren't other schools having to share therapists? In one case, a principal honestly believed that the reduction in first-grade teachers was "retribution" for voicing a dissenting opinion at a cabinet meeting three years earlier, not the large drop in first graders at the school.

As friends of these "unfairly" targeted staff ramp up the pressure to protect their colleagues from an arbitrary central office, a somewhat beleaguered superintendent tries to explain the logic behind the decisions. Unfortunately, the din is loud, not many are listening, and the calculations can seem like weak justification. The same rules, applied in advance, depersonalize the decision and lower anxiety and pushback.

All sorts of guidelines can help break staffing stickiness; for example:

- Elementary grade levels in a school can have only x number of teachers for a given level of enrollment. Rather than just setting targets, such as 25 students per class, policy predetermines staffing levels in the gray areas, such as how many teachers if there are 101 students, 102, 103, and so on. What to do when enrollment isn't evenly divisible by 25 is already answered.
- Teaching load guidelines at the secondary level might provide one social studies teacher for every 115 students taking social studies. When course enrollment drops from 950 to 825 students, everyone is expecting one social studies position to be cut, shifted, or repurposed.

- Setting the expectation for one ELL teacher per thirty-five ELL students, for example, automatically moves staff between schools as the number of English language learners changes over time.
- If one full-time equivalent (FTE) special educator or speech therapist is assigned to a school for every, say, twenty hours of direct instructional groups required by IEPs, this provides much-needed staffing flexibility and precision.
- If guidelines dictate that elementary schools get one art teacher for every twenty-five homerooms, then a school with eighteen homerooms would expect to have a shared or part-time teacher.

Guidelines like these automatically cut, move, or add staff each year and encourage staff being shared between schools when appropriate, but they do even more to change a district's culture. In these districts, changes to curriculum are easier, or changes to leadership roles and responsibilities go more smoothly. These districts have built a culture of fluidity. Change is normal.

PAY MORE ATTENTION TO SECONDARY SCHOOLS

At the secondary level, course offerings and teaching load can become inflexible like class size at the elementary level, and changes can bring much pushback from teachers, department heads, and principals. In many districts, elementary school staffing is reviewed each year under a microscope, but high school staffing gets only a quick, distant glance. In some districts, the number of elementary classrooms (and thus the number of elementary teachers) is carefully set each year based on actual enrollment. If King Elementary School has fewer first graders one year, one section is dropped. This approach builds some flexibility and efficiency into budgeting; principals, teachers, and parents expect such a cut, because it's automatic and rule-based. In the same district, however, it's common that high school staffing is much harder to change. Often the unofficial practice and expectation is "everyone comes back." High schools that normalize the idea that the teaching force is constant, regardless of student course enrollment, create barriers to budget changes.

For example, in one district the culture of high school staff stability led to very wasteful spending and fierce resistance to passing a smarter budget. As students opted for more foreign language and science electives, fewer students signed up for family and consumer science—the modern name for home economics. Classes like sewing, baking, and health had declining enrollments. Over time, 60 percent fewer students were taking these classes, but staffing remained constant at 4.0 FTE. When the superintendent proposed cutting out 1.5 positions, a firestorm erupted. The public felt it unfair to "target one department" or to "punish hardworking veteran staff." The debate centered on stability for these teachers who had the implicit expectation of job security, regardless of student need. Despite tight budgets, all four teachers remained; only retirement in the following years brought the department into alignment with course enrollment. Some districts avoid this battle by creating staffing guidelines based on teaching load. They set clear expectations that each teacher will serve, say, 125 students (5 classes of 25). If only 250 students sign up for family and consumer science, then just 2.0 FTE will be funded. Such a practice creates the expectation that staffing matches enrollment, and de-personalizes the decision, making it more palatable.

In a number of detailed studies conducted by my firm, the majority of middle and high schools had some departments overstaffed due to shifting enrollment and often at least one department understaffed. The schools were more likely to add staff as course enrollment increased, but the desire for stability in staffing led to some very overburdened departments as well. More students didn't always lead to more staff, just bigger classes and stressed teachers. In the district with too many family and consumer science teachers, Latin teachers each taught up to 160 students (versus 60 in family and consumer science) and often moved to other districts for relief.

Middle schools can pose a special challenge when it comes to flexibility in staffing. In many districts the so-called middle school model is a third-rail budget topic. Middle schools replaced junior highs starting more than forty years ago. As a norm, the middle school model creates grade-level teams of students, say one hundred kids, who all share the same math, English, science, and social studies teacher, creating a "small school within a school" atmosphere. Some people love this concept (especially middle school teachers), while some think it's flawed and worry students attending traditional middle schools underachieve compared to K–8, but that is a debate for another book.[1] The rigidity of executing the middle school model, if a district opts for it, is the issue at hand.

For schools with 100 or 200 (or any multiple of 100) students per grade, the classic middle school staffing pattern works fine. Each teacher on a team teaches four classes a day, has one prep period, and has a team meeting with his or her teacher teammates. Inherent to this plan is that teachers teach only one grade level and are part of one team. Issues arise when enrollment doesn't neatly match this plan. With, say, 175 students per grade, a school might have more teachers than actually needed because only seven sections are required for each subject per grade, but 2.0 full-time staff, who can teach eight classes total, will be hired.

As enrollment changes from year to year, many districts find that even small changes to middle school staffing or schedules unleash a torrent of concern from teachers that the model is under attack. Some districts have created greater flexibility and acceptance to changed staffing by making clear statements about their commitment to the middle school model, and defining which key elements they hold dear and which can change. This includes:

- content teachers serving more than one grade when enrollment dictates;
- team meetings being held less than daily to provide more instructional time; and
- some teacher meetings by department, not team, to review data and share best practices.

Creating a clear definition of what will be fixed and what can vary from year to year can better serve middle school students and the budget.

Staffing guidelines bring flexibility to staffing and create a culture that shifts other spending more easily as well. Not to worry: these districts aren't wild merry-go-rounds of staff moving every year, with no ties, bonds, or friendships formed. Often, just a few teachers out of a hundred are impacted each year, but that's enough to free up significant funds for strategic priorities and build a culture that's more comfortable with change.

INCREASE CLASS SIZE WITH LESS PARENT AND TEACHER ANXIETY

Few budget battles are as fierce as increasing class size. Parents, teachers, and principals prefer smaller classes. Yet class size is perhaps the biggest controllable variable in a district budget. Small increases in class size can free up big dollars for strategic priorities, or close budget gaps with little impact on student outcomes. If the freed-up funds are put to good use, slightly bigger classes can lead to big achievement gains. Perhaps the most common question I'm asked is, "How do I build support for increasing class size?" Many superintendents have tried and failed.

The most striking example of embedding flexibility into resource decisions is how differently districts manage the always-contentious issue of class size. Most districts have class size guidelines. They vary greatly from district to district. In some schools, twenty-two students in K–2 is the max; for others, it's twenty-eight. Some consider a high school class of twenty-five the target, while others say thirty-two. These types of class size guidelines come in a number of styles. They may be maximums or loose targets, or hardwired into collective bargaining agreements. Whatever the flavor, the targets are visible, unambiguous, and easy to understand.

Oddly, this clarity creates a problem. Any change in class size is thus very visible and often becomes a flash point with parents, teachers, and principals. Even when the guidelines are nonbinding, they can be very restrictive. In one district, the "target" was twenty-four students for elementary classrooms. One small school had fifty third graders, up from just forty-four the year before. The district opted for two classrooms of twenty-five, just one student over the nonbinding target. While legally, contractually, or morally this didn't break any rule, it crossed a cultural line in the sand. Parent outrage ensued. After four face-to-face meetings with angry parents, and two uncomfortable public budget forums, the superintendent relented—sort of. The two classes would share a teaching assistant and a student teacher. This calmed no one. The end of the story is well known to many who have tried to increase class size: three classes of sixteen and seventeen were created, costing the district $70,000.

This "one more is just too many" feeling was widespread even though:

- the two existing third-grade teachers were very strong;
- the following year, only two sections would be needed;
- adding the extra classroom teacher would eliminate funding for a reading teacher in the school; and
- the average class size in the school was only twenty-two students.

This didn't matter. Twenty-four students was considered "normal," and thus twenty-five seemed wrong. It was as if the class size discussion was ringed with police tape proclaiming "do not cross."

Contrast this story to one of the more flexible districts. It raised class size by one to two students in hundreds of elementary classrooms with little protest. The difference was the district had intentionally moved away from simple, clear targets. It had a more complex formula. Lower grades had smaller classes, but higher income schools in the district had bigger classes. Teachers with top track records of student growth had bigger classes, while novice teachers had slightly smaller ones. Principals had and regularly used autonomy to increase class size a bit to add social workers or other supports. The effect was that class sizes varied greatly from school to school, grade to grade, and year to year. Parents came to expect ever-changing class sizes. Some years there might be eighteen students in a class, but other years there were many more. The school community didn't have highly visible, "do not cross this line under penalty of death" expectations.

A less radical approach to creating more flexibility around class size is to shift to guidelines that target *average* class size, not *maximum* class size. This may seem a bit technical, but it's a big difference both financially and culturally. On the financial side, hard caps can raise the costs of staffing a school by 5 percent or more. In very small schools the extra cost can easily exceed 10 percent. Here's how: An elementary school with class size maximums of twenty-five must have three classes if fifty-one students are in a grade, but only two if there are fifty students. The addition of one student adds one teacher, plus one more section of PE, art, music, and library since this extra classroom will also go to a separate special class period each day.

On the other hand, if districts target an average, not a maximum, of twenty-five students in a class, then if one grade averaged twenty-five and a half students, and another averaged twenty-four and a half, all is well and one less teacher would be required.

The cultural benefit of setting target class sizes based on an average may be even bigger than the financial benefit. When some grades might have twenty-two students, and others twenty-seven, one year, and the opposite is true the following year, students (and their teachers and parents) experience varying class size, and thus the class size target is less visible and less likely to become a sacred cow. It's obvious to all and more likely a flash point when the cap is raised from twenty-four to twenty-five because every teacher with twenty-five students—and parents with students in these classes—knows that without the change, the class would have been smaller. It crossed a line in the sand. As with any good idea, thoughtful implementation matters. Districts with class size averages tend to keep kindergarten and first grade small, and if third grade was big one year, they make sure that fourth grade isn't the next year.

In many districts, elementary special classes are both hard to change and unchanging (a related phenomenon). Students go to one special class each day, typically on a five-day weekly cycle, such as art once a week, PE twice a week, and so on. Each homeroom class goes to one special at a time. This is such a well-established pattern in most districts that some will wonder what flexibility is possible or even desired. In tough economic times some districts have tried to cut back on elementary art and music and, reasonably so, a parent firestorm ensues. Parents should be disappointed, because not providing such programs isn't a case of doing more with less, it's just doing less. Interestingly, many other options are possible to keep these important offerings and reduce their costs if needed, if districts embrace a more flexible approach to staffing, scheduling, and class size.

Changing the cycle year to year can help free up funds and create flexibility to respond to changing enrollment. It's a bit technical, but efficient scheduling can require specials to be on a three-, four-, or five-day cycle, depending on school enrollment. On a four-day cycle, for example, students have a special every day, but the topic repeats every four days instead of every week—no big deal for students, but staffing costs can drop because specials teachers can be scheduled more efficiently. In some districts the specials cycle changes from year to year or school to school. In many districts, however, such a change would be as odd as moving Thanksgiving to a Tuesday in October.

Flexibility in elementary specials happens along a few dimensions. Some districts send multiple classes to a special at once, perhaps three classes to PE and one and a half to art (the other half of the class joins yet another half-class in the library). As budgets and staffing levels change, so can the decision on how many classes should attend for each section. In all the options, students get the same services, but costs do vary.

Finally, some districts normalize creating flexibility in how much FTE is assigned to each school and sharing specials teachers among schools, thus ensuring every teacher teaches a full load, which can reduce costs without reducing programming. This is in contrast to the fairly common approach of having one (or two) specialists per school, a practice that can harden into an intractable commitment. In one large district facing $20 million in budget cuts, an analysis revealed that $1 million could be saved if elementary specials teachers who didn't have a full teaching load were shared between schools. This seemed just too odd to principals and central office, and basically unfair, so they cut other programs rather than "make specials teachers travel between schools," a practice that is completely normal elsewhere.

BE FLEXIBLE ABOUT BUS AND SCHOOL ASSIGNMENTS

My phone didn't stop ringing and parents didn't stop shouting, sometimes hysterically. What brought on these aggressive calls? The school committee, on which I served, had voted to trim two buses from the fleet because ridership was down. The panic-stricken parents noted, with alarm, that some bus stops had moved (down a few driveways), pickup times changed (plus or minus ten minutes), and the bus route number would be different (seriously: "Johnny always rides bus 14"). Having fewer buses meant lots of changes to the stops on almost every route in an effort to avoid lengthening the average ride to school. The pushback was intense, and hastily one bus was brought back into service as a peace offering.

This $100,000-savings-turned-political-nightmare was a stark case of having normalized the status quo. The district practice was to hardly ever change bus routes and stops. Yes, we added new ones as needed, but we didn't alter existing ones. Sometimes two stops might be just a few driveways apart. The lesson was clear: we needed a new, more flexible way of managing transportation, and we needed to get parents more comfortable with change. The board decided that clear rules and guidelines would help and that updating the routes and stops each year based on these guidelines would prevent future pushback, not repeat it. The routes, pickup times, and bus numbers did change again, every year in fact, but they changed in the years that didn't have cuts to the fleet as well. In the years that followed, buses continued to be trimmed every few years as enrollment dropped, but without the parent outcry.

Some districts normalize flexibility in transportation to an even higher level. At middle schools and high schools, afternoon runs are different than morning runs, because so many students stay for afterschool sports or clubs. They even change it up seasonally, based on extracurricular participation. Yet other districts regularly modify the routes about two weeks into the school year based on actual ridership data.

In all these cases, the flexibility saved money in the current budget, but it also created room to maneuver in the future to make more changes to transportation without parent push-back. Finally, when most aspects of a district change annually, not arbitrarily but based on data and guidelines, the overall culture becomes more accepting of change.

Getting parents comfortable with change can be taken to a very high level in districts that have flexible school assignment practices. If I hadn't learned about it firsthand, I would never have believed it. Having grown up just a few houses away from "my" school and having watched the fierce, heated battles (typically lost) to close or redistrict schools, I had long assumed that there could be little flexibility in school assignments for students. It's hard to move a house or a school, so a district can't easily manage which children attend which schools, I figured. On both political and logistical grounds, school assignment zones seemed as fixed as the roads that define the boundaries.

Given the emotional anguish that accompanies any tinkering with which school children attend, there ought to be one hell of a good reason to even think about messing with it. Actually, there *can* be a very good reason. Efficient staffing and class size management are the single biggest drivers of district budgets, and are most efficient when students come to school in nice, evenly divisible batches of, say, twenty-four, or whatever the target class size is. Obviously, they don't. In a district with firm class size rules (set by policy or state law) forty-eight students at a school in a grade means two teachers, but forty-nine means three. One extra student added roughly $75,000 to the budget.

In districts where realtors include the neighborhood school's stats in home listings, and the attendance boundaries change at a geological pace, even forming a redistricting study committee can pack a school board meeting and derail the effort before it's started.

A number of large districts have found ways to normalize very flexible definitions of a "close to home" school. One district with class caps managed its schools a lot like how hotels manage their rooms. If you call up and ask for a room, and the hotel is full, they don't build you a new room. This district, with reasonably high student mobility, allowed new students to enroll in a school only if there was room in an existing class. Students who moved into such a district didn't automatically go to the nearest school. They were assigned based on availability of open seats. This is a very effective strategy for districts with high mobility. To be sure, such a strategy leads to efficient staffing, but it also leads to much flexibility in budgeting in other areas. The district's assignment policy sent a strong message to staff and the community: We are very prudent with your tax dollars. We carefully manage staffing and enrollment, and there are few guarantees. Change is normal in this district.

Another district took a very sophisticated approach to define a home school—actually, home *schools*. Every single house in the district had six choice schools based on proximity. A house just down the street might have a slightly different mix, if it was closer to another school. In this case, rather than having a dozen or so fixed zones, which were impossible to change, the district had thousands of zones and some choice for all. In both cases, once at a school, the student was guaranteed a seat in future years.

While urban schools—with lots of schools, school options, and strategies of school choice—are an easier fit for this approach, some suburban districts have also created more flexibility in school boundaries in an effort to normalize "annual redistricting" as part of class size management. They created *buffer zones*, neighborhoods in which students can be assigned *by the district* to one of two schools, as shown in figure 1.1.

FIGURE 1.1
Enrollment buffer zones make managing class size easier

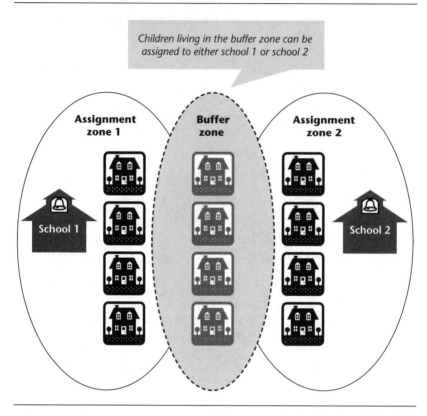

Parents can indicate their preference, but the district makes the final decision based on its desire to balance class size. Again, once students were assigned, future placements weren't in doubt. The district purposely rejected simply making new boundaries to address big swings in enrollment, because the problem of over- and underutilized schools had flourished for more than a decade but was too politically charged to address. Only a state requirement to increase enrollment at one school prompted the redistricting, but the superintendent specifically wanted to create flexibility in the future, each year normalizing shifting attendance patterns for students entering school for the first time.

Normalizing change through staffing guidelines, policies, and practices that make managing and raising class size easier, and by regularly shifting building assignments as student needs shift, creates more cost-effective staffing and a culture that accepts all changes more easily.

2

BUILD A VISION BEFORE
BUILDING A BUDGET

*Forging a Common Plan for What the Future
Should Look Like Makes It Easier to Rally Around
a Budget That Leads to That Future*

Imagine the horror. A man born to wealthy slave owners turns on his country and leads an armed revolt, killing many loyal citizens, even attacking the unsuspecting on Christmas Eve. While he was vilified by many in England at the time, we Americans revere him as our founding father and our very popular first president. It seems the line between villain and hero depends on where you live. There is an important lesson here for those hoping to do more with less in school districts across the nation forged by George Washington.

Too often those leading the charge to improve student outcomes through shifts in spending feel they have the moral high ground. I have certainly fallen into this trap. When I was superintendent, I was friends with a teacher in the district, and over dinner commented that I'm sure she saw the value of a new math plan, since we typically agreed on most issues. Looking away, she quietly said, "You're an ass, and dead wrong." I'm not sure I was either of these, but I definitely was surprised.

The desire to fund a new reading program (a great goal) by cutting home economics, very small classes, or tutors, for example, can feel like a morally righteous effort, and it's easy to dismiss those opposed as just recalcitrant, status-quo-loving union members putting the needs of adults before kids. But thinking that those who oppose budget cuts, shifts, and redeployment just don't care as much about student outcomes is wrong and shortsighted, and undermines gaining support for bold budget changes.

Very often the source of resistance to change isn't a lack of caring for kids, or putting the needs of the organization ahead of students, but rather sincere, heartfelt differences in beliefs. These differences stem from having alternative definitions of success or theories of action for achieving success. By first building a shared vision and shared beliefs, district leaders can help close the divide and build support for smarter budgets.

After participating in more than a hundred budget battles as a school board member, district administrator, or consultant, I think the root cause of much of the pushback stems from leaders butting up against these sincere differences in beliefs about what will actually help students and what the end goal for students really is. In this chapter we'll dig deeper into how to align beliefs, create a shared vision, and win support for bolder budgets.

CONFRONT HEAD-ON DIFFERING MEASURES OF SUCCESS

At a high level, we all want the same thing for our students: health, happiness, a good career, and the ability to be an informed citizen. At the next layer down, we as a nation start to diverge. President Obama has angered some in his own party with his call for college for all. Some believe a technical vocation is an equally lofty goal.

When we get down to much more day-to-day measures of success, the differences of opinion can be large. We all agree on the importance of reading, but whether second graders should read at a developmental reading assessment (DRA) level of 14 or 18 doesn't have the same degree of consensus. Sure, math is important, but should students with mild special needs master Algebra I or a more basic "math concepts" class? A state English language arts test that emphasizes grammar and vocabulary might not seem important to a teacher who values writing and higher-order thinking skills. Why do these differences of opinion matter to passing smarter budgets? Because most shifts in resources are intended to address a need. Otherwise, why bother moving funds? If key stakeholders don't see a need, there is little chance they will support the shift.

I failed to appreciate this when I first became superintendent. A quick review of the data showed that 68 percent of students were reading on grade level, and far fewer students with special needs, who came from poverty, or who were learning English. I was alarmed: I was failing one-third of our students. Bold action was needed, and sweeping shifts in spending were proposed. I actually expected much appreciation for finding the dollars to address this burning need. Many stakeholders saw the situation differently:

- More than half of all students were proficient. That's not bad.
- Many of the struggling readers had disabilities or parents who didn't read to them at home. It's not really

reasonable to expect them to read at the same level as "regular kids."

- The state doesn't set reading levels in K–2, so district-reported low proficiency in these grades must be because we set our internal bar too high.

While I, and some of my leadership team, saw our results as a call to action, many did not. Lacking support to move forward, I stepped back from the budget battle and started months of dialogue with principals, board members, and key influencers in the central office and schools. We began by trying to surface what we defined as success. This wasn't a casual one-off conversation. We hired a third-party facilitator, did Outward Bound bonding exercises, used confidential means of sharing our thoughts (through SurveyMonkey), and engaged in hours of large-group, small-group, and private conversations. This still wasn't enough to align our definitions of success. Guest speakers, case studies, a few conferences, and joint discussions of the research ultimately did lead to a shared belief that 95 percent of all students should read at grade level, based on the highest nationally normed standard we could find.

With a shared determination to get every student to mastery, and more importantly, a shared definition of mastery, dollars and actions started to shift. The next two budgets cut dozens of line items, programs, and, unfortunately, administrators and teachers so that we could add reading teachers, instructional coaches, intensive summer training institutes, data analysts, and more. These changes were strongly supported and became bedrock in the district, because we all agreed we had a problem that should, could, and must be addressed.

A side benefit of having a shared measure of success up front was that as scores started to rise, no one questioned the effectiveness or importance of the changes. Five years later, nearly 93 percent of all K–5 students read on grade level, just shy of our goal, and despite many subsequent rounds of budget cuts, nearly all the investment in reading remains intact.

With hindsight, I see how caring, smart people can disagree on what constitutes success for a student, especially when it relies on state tests or includes students with extra challenges. Some state tests set a low bar, prioritize fill-in-the blank memorization, and skip writing or complex thinking. Even the best test doesn't yet measure emotional well-being, empathy, the ability to work in groups, resilience, or other important outcomes. Letting shared beliefs drive agreement on the budget means not limiting what's important to the things currently measured, but rather measuring what's considered important.

Some areas that address common basic beliefs but lack readily available measures include:

- reading in grades K–3 (most state tests start at the end of grade 3);
- socialization of students served in inclusive settings;
- team work;
- higher-order thinking;
- creativity and artistic expression; and
- grit, hard work, and resilience.

The other pitfall that seems to entrap many superintendents (including me) and school board members (including me) is assuming that state and federal mandates are important to everyone else. It's part of the leader's job to abide by all regulations, policies (such as having a balanced budget), or requirements (such as meeting NCLB proficiency targets). In fact, failure to do so can have extreme repercussions—being fired for overspending, or facing sanctions and state interventions for low achievement. These consequences can focus a leader's attention! Unfortunately, parents, teachers, and even some principals don't find policy and mandates very compelling reasons to support unpleasant decisions.

One superintendent facing a huge budget gap proposed thoughtful, targeted, student-centered cuts to balance the budget. His message to the community was, "These are deep but necessary cuts. We must match expenses to revenue." While that message was true, it wasn't inspiring. Every cut created a core group of opponents, and few rallied to support having less. Bewildered, the superintendent carefully explained state law on the need for a balanced budget and presented charts showing a declining tax base. This was compelling to him, but most stakeholders felt that the district should just find more money. A balanced budget wasn't a strong call to action. Most wanted the proposed cuts restored. In the end, having gained little agreement on what was important, the district opted for across-the-board cuts—the least strategic option available.

Values vary by district. In some locales, having a balanced budget, being frugal, and living within your means are shared values and carry more weight.

"Because the state said so" is also often not a unifying message. In the early days of No Child Left Behind, shifting resources to grades or subjects that scored low on the new state test seemed logical. If middle school math is underperforming, shifting some dollars to computerized intervention should draw support. Unfortunately, in many districts, few teachers embraced the state tests, and thus wouldn't sacrifice much to improve these results. When the conversation shifted to ensuring that all students master college-ready math, support grew. The Common Core may present a similar challenge.

UNDERSTAND DIFFERING (IMPLICIT) THEORIES OF ACTION

Budget battles can be so intense because the stakes are high. The stakes are high because children's futures hang in the balance, and nearly everyone cares about kids and no one wants to do wrong by them. Oddly, this shared passion leads to some of the most divisive fights. So how does a common desire to help lead to brutal, knock-down disagreements? It's not just differing definitions of success; it's often differing beliefs of how to achieve success that fuels many budget battles.

A person's beliefs on how best to raise achievement or provide a meaningful education are, in edu-speak jargon, his or her *theory of action*. A theory of action is often phrased as a series of if-then statements that spell out causal relationships of logic, and is often based on deep-seated instinct. Let's compare three reasonable but opposing theories of action:

1. If teachers are given the freedom to meet the individual needs of their students, and if teachers are provided adequate time to plan and differentiate instruction, then all children will be well served and achievement will increase.
2. If proven best practices are uniformly applied with fidelity and if practice is regularly modified based on real-time student growth results, then effective practices will spread widely and be fine-tuned regularly, all children will be well served, and achievement will increase.
3. If individual student needs are identified and instruction is personalized for both learning style and skill level, then all children will be well served and achievement will increase.

None of these is crazy or extreme. But each is different, and that can be a big problem during budget time. Imagine a cocktail party of principals, central office folks, and school board members milling around with drinks in hand, hors d'oeuvres being passed, and light conversation bandied about.

"I really like how my teachers get to know their students so well," says a principal. "They differentiate their lessons often."

"Yes," says a board member, "my son just loves science and has recently explored the Goddard Space Flight Museum in the computer lab."

"It's wonderful when all teachers allow students to select topics that interest them," chimes in the reading director.

The conversation pauses as each grabs a meatball on a frilly toothpick, and it's hard to imagine this pleasant, agreeable conversation leading to shouting, name calling, and personal attacks in a different setting—but it can.

Now imagine these same people in the conference room next to the superintendent's office, wrestling with next year's budget, which calls for trimming spending a bit and highlights a growing need to close the rich-poor achievement gap.

"We must maintain our small class size if teachers are going to be able to know their students. It's impossible to differentiate instruction if there are twenty-five students in a room. If we want to help students of poverty, then we must further reduce class size," the principal, who believes differentiation is key, says heatedly, angry that a proposal to increase class size is being seriously considered.

"It's quality, not quantity!" the central office administrator, who is focusing on fidelity to the district plans, says a bit too loudly. "The research on class size is clear. Our teachers are good, but too many aren't implementing the curriculum with fidelity.

We need an instructional coach in each school and means to monitor instructional practices."

"Yes, I understand, but our computers are six years old, and we must upgrade our technology. The iPad wasn't even invented the last time we bought technology in my son's school," complains the tech-favoring board member.

When dollars are in short supply, differing theories of action can drive a wedge between people with similar goals and create much pushback for any given spending plan. Fortunately, there are a number of ways of managing and reducing the pushback caused by differing theories of action.

Recognize That Everyone Has a Theory of Action

Most people's theory of action is more subconscious than overt. They may never formally articulate it, even to themselves, but they are strongly guided by it.

Perhaps the most common unstated theories of action include the belief in the benefit of small class sizes, the utility of paraprofessionals to help struggling students, and the value of more dollars for the classroom and less for administration.

Often, discussions about specific budget line items are in fact surrogate debates of underlying implicit theories of action. The discussion of whether to add or reduce instructional coaches, for example, hinges not just on the effectiveness of the current coaching effort or the needs of teachers, but also on a debate about what strategy is best for raising achievement—class size versus managed instruction versus technology, and so on. Continuing with our example, when the school board member says, "Our current coaching hasn't been very helpful," the statement is often strongly influenced by her desire for more technology, rather than the job description or performance of the coaches.

It's very helpful to bring into the open implicit theories of action. It is easier and more productive to discuss competing theories of action than to wage proxy battles over various line-item spending levels. There are two ways of surfacing an individual's implicit theory of action.

The first is to just ask, but in a very safe and structured way. I have led many retreats that allowed administrative cabinets, school boards, and building principals to identify, and then discuss, their underlying beliefs about what it takes to raise achievement. The basic agenda starts with a review of what a theory of action is and explains that there are many valid and differing ones. (See "Theories of Action: Aligning Priorities and Resources" in the fall 2011 *District Management Journal* for a good prereading exercise and a full list of common theories of action.) The next step is to list all the likely elements of common theories of action, as shown in the partial list in table 2.1.

At this point, participants are asked to privately select up to five elements they think are key to raising achievement and providing a meaningful education. No discussion is allowed yet.

Next we go public. Participants each get five green stickers to place their votes on a poster-sized chart of the list of options. For an added twist, you can provide three red stickers to indicate potential elements of theories of action that participants believe are contrary to the research base.

At this point we have made visible the (sometimes very conflicting) beliefs of everyone in the room. The importance of elementary reading is often a top vote getter, but beyond that it's common to see wide variation and outright differences of opinion, with lots of green and red dots on the same choice, such as small class size or technology. Now a more reasoned discussion of which theory of action should drive the district's spending can begin.

TABLE 2.1
Selected common components of theory of action for raising achievement

Staff-driven elements:

1. *Principal autonomy*: Shifting resource allocation and decision making to the building level—where employees are most equipped to make decisions that benefit children—will increase student achievement.

2. *Teacher quality*: Setting expectations for what is "effective teaching," and providing frequent feedback to teachers through classroom observations and verbal feedback, will improve teacher instructional practice and increase student achievement.

3. *Performance compensation*: Providing incentives for strong performance will increase motivation for improvement, attract stronger candidates to working in education, and increase student achievement.

Organizational and cultural elements

4. *Professional learning communities*: Frequent collaboration among teachers in a grade or subject will improve instructional practice and increase student achievement.

5. *Systems thinking*: By combining multiple theories of change, all of which reinforce and logically connect to each other, all district decisions, practices, and resources will support a coherent set of beliefs that will raise student achievement.

6. *High expectations*: Increasing and standardizing expectations for students or staff will push them harder to achieve great things, creating a culture of high performance and increasing teacher effectiveness and/or student achievement.

Curriculum-based elements

7. *Standards-based and data-driven*: Setting clear standards, measuring progress through the use of common formative assessments, and frequently reviewing student achievement data will improve instructional practice and increase student achievement.

8. *Managed instruction*: A districtwide curriculum, coupled with pacing guides and related professional development, will provide a seamless and aligned system of learning across the district, and lead to increases in student achievement.

9. *Whole child*: Engaging students in the visual and performing arts, physical education and athletics, and career and technical education will increase student engagement in school, build confidence, and increase student achievement.

Structural elements

10. *Small class size*: Providing smaller class sizes will make classroom management easier, better equip teachers to meet individual student needs, and increase student achievement.

11. *Technology-rich*: Increasing the use of technology and connecting schools with the outside world through the Internet will increase student motivation and help students more effectively gain twenty-first-century skills.

12. *More time*: Providing more time on task in critical subject areas, either through extended school hours, a lengthened school year, or by borrowing time from less critical subjects, will increase student learning.

A more interactive, technology-infused way to surface often-buried theories of action is by using a computerized budget-building simulation. In this approach, key stakeholders are tasked with balancing a budget and funding new efforts for a fictitious school district that surprisingly is similar in size, student demographics, and per-pupil spending as their own. Dealing with a fictitious district facing a budget crunch and desire to improve student outcomes surfaces people's true values, because their decisions in the simulation don't impact friends and colleagues. One such simulation was developed by my firm, the District Management Council.

The simulation asks stakeholders to balance the shrinking budget and provides them with the option to cut deeper to fund investments in new initiatives. Over one hundred choices are provided—reducing paraprofessionals, increasing class size in high school electives, raising fees for extracurriculars, cutting back on professional development, increasing health-care copays, and adding instructional coaches or reading teachers, to name just a few. As each selection is made, the impact on the budget is instantly calculated.

Another benefit of a good budget simulator is that it changes the discussion from good or bad to better or worse—that is, it moves from absolute judgments to relative trade-offs. Sure, bigger classes aren't good. No one *wants* bigger classes, but what's more valuable, slightly bigger classes in exchange for one data analyst? Twenty-five reading teachers? The answer might be "Not worth it for one person in the central office, but now if we could really get twenty-five additional reading teachers, that's a different story."

Good budget simulators force real-world trade-offs by calculating the actual financial impact of different decisions. I'm amazed how often participants, somewhat gleefully, point out that the simulator is broken, because it shows that adding one student to a high school class or each special ed or reading intervention group saves millions, when they were certain it saves just thousands! But it *does* free up millions of dollars in a district of their size. Many participants are equally dismayed to learn that increasing health insurance copays or deductibles moves manyfold more dollars than gutting central office, out-of-state travel, and association dues combined. It's common to hear mutterings like "This is hard" and "I had no idea." Experiencing and experimenting with trade-offs in a safe setting helps stakeholders set the stage for doing it with their own budgets. It also makes it easier to support many seemingly harsh decisions.

Forcing participants to make hard choices and explain their thinking to their teammates quickly, and safely, surfaces personal values and competing theories of action.

Now that you've surfaced the theories of action of the key stakeholders, it's beneficial to discuss the differences of opinion prior to rolling up your sleeves to build a budget. The discussion is more honest and productive. In one district, among seventeen cabinet members more than a dozen competing theories of action emerged, such as a focus on tight central office control, principal empowerment, the importance of the arts, and a hyperfocus on elementary reading. It came as no surprise that past budgets left everyone feeling bruised, insulted, and dissatisfied. It also explained why across-the-board cuts or not replacing whichever staff member left (the least strategic of decisions) were the norm.

With the help of a facilitator, over the course of four or five half-day sessions, they forged a broad consensus. Reading was job one and best practices did exist, but principals and teachers with above-average growth would have freedom from some districtwide practices, so long as student growth remained high. Also, time for the arts would be maintained, but lower-cost options would be considered if they didn't reduce student time in the arts. Interestingly, the leadership team did not feel they had the time for such "philosophical" discussions, but they always found much, much more time to fight over the budget.

With the team now unified by a common theory of action, building the next budget was both strategic and relatively peaceful. Reading teachers and instructional coaches were added, and data systems improved, all funded by shifting to some part-time arts teachers (no reduction in student time in the arts, but if a school needed only 0.8 FTE it got only 0.8 FTE, rather than a full-time teacher with some extra prep periods) and sweeping realignment of Title I and IIa grants. Over the next few years, reading scores skyrocketed. Seven years later, most of these changes remain because the theory of action served as a guiding light and North Star.

Create a Safe Space for Candid Conversation

Making the best use of limited dollars, ending popular but ineffective programs, and shifting staffing based on student need all require some technical skill, but they also require a lot of open, honest dialogue. A desire for outward politeness, oft-valued in many districts, prevents open and thoughtful debate on underlying values and beliefs embedded in differing theories of action.

Differences of opinion are not hidden so much as masqueraded. The attack is often from the flank, not head-on. Stakeholders say, "The contract doesn't allow larger classes," or "We can't build a schedule with one less middle school team." But this interaction skirts the underlying debate—differing beliefs about class size. When well facilitated, a candid discussion of differing values, beliefs, and resulting theories of action yields two good things. The first is that honestly discussing differences can help build trust and understanding, whereas the flanking attacks often infuriate others and breed animosity.

Better yet, such a discussion can reveal previously unknown areas of agreement. I have watched diametrically opposed sides find middle ground. "Well, yes, I'm okay with larger classes in _____ (high school, music and PE, fifth grade, etc.) but not in _____ (elementary, intervention, K–3, etc.)" or "Well, if we are not reducing hours of service to kids with IEPs, but just streamlining meetings and paperwork, then I guess we could reduce some special education staff." Understanding the nuances of people's beliefs—where the boundaries lie exactly—makes it easy to create plans that align with these values.

Candid conversation about what's important between administrators and the leaders and the district helps create internal support for bolder shifts in resources. Candor with the school board can also be very helpful, but creating a safe place for principals and other administrators to speak openly with the school board is hard in a system of open meeting laws and public document requests. George Carlin had his list of seven words you can't say on TV (that was before cable, of course), and likewise some things are just hard to say with reporters and the public in the room.

In many states it's perfectly on the up and up to have school board informational sessions with less than a quorum of the board present. Typically no decision can be made or even deliberated. Some districts bring principals to these meetings to share more candidly their support for tough decisions and the rationale for the change. A less "in the spotlight" opportunity can encourage principals to be advocates. An alternative is the offsite board retreat, perhaps using the budget simulator with principals and central office staff participating as well.

Realize Strategic Planning Can Help or Hurt

Many districts turn to strategic planning as a means to codify an agreed-upon theory of action. Conventional wisdom says the budget is the financial representation of a district's strategic plan. In the best of cases it is, but in the worst of cases—it is! When a strategic plan is grounded in a theory of action, spells out a few key changes needed to embrace the theory of action, and shifts resources accordingly, it can lead to much learning and minimal fighting over the budget.

Often, however, strategic planning accelerates budget battles rather than ends them. A much too common approach to strategic planning unintentionally makes focused, strategic budgeting nearly impossible. In an effort to engage the community, the district or a consultant hired to help holds a series of public forums. In a world of social networking, these forums are often augmented by online chats, text-ins, SurveyMonkey, and Facebook pages to be more inclusive. The public is asked some variation of "What's key to preserve, what's not working, and what do we need new or more of?" If one hundred people respond, one hundred wish lists for spending emerge, and if one thousand respond, one thousand wish lists are collected: smaller classes, fewer administrators, Chinese language, more JV sports, higher-order thinking, shorter bus rides, new computers, and so on. This process often skips creating an actionable theory of action, instead opting for a broad, aspirational but nondirective one, something on the order of:

> If all teachers engage with their students and are supported by collaboration, are guided by data, and receive relevant and

embedded professional development, while working in a caring community of professionals; and if students are engaged in a rigorous curriculum that's both aligned to standards and relevant to their lives; and if all students partake in a wide array of arts and athletics, then all students will be ready for college and successful careers as thoughtful citizens of a multicultural democracy.

This is a Rorschach theory of action. As with the inkblot images, the beholder can see whatever he is pre-inclined to see.

One district, aided by a well-respected firm, created a strategic plan listing 147 needs for more this, that, and other stuff. The facts that district expenses were already growing faster than revenue and layoffs were looming didn't shorten the lists provided by engaged, enthused, and appreciative-to-have-a-voice stakeholders. In an effort to create some focus, they designated 53 items as first priority. As the next budget was built, stakeholders could each point to the strategic plan for why their area of concern should receive more funding. In the end, most stakeholders felt betrayed, because when small across-the-board cuts were made, they felt all of their hard work on the strategic plan was ignored.

To be sure, public engagement and strategic planning are important, but in a world of declining resources, the process must lead to prioritization, not proliferation, of needed changes driven by a concise, unambiguous theory of action.

A more constructive approach can lead to financial peace and student gains. One district of roughly ten thousand students serves as a great example.

This context seems an unlikely setting for a happy ending. The district was experiencing a significant demographic shift, as its student population became browner and poorer, at the time that dramatic revenue shortfalls were forecast. Over the next few years spending would drop by more than $15 million, about 10 percent of the operating budget. To further complicate matters, the school board was fractured and contentious, representing a split between the old and new demographics of the community, with a bit of Tea Party versus Big Government divergence as well. It should be no surprise that budget discussions were mean-spirited, draining ordeals that resulted in just less of the same.

The district, in frustration, decided to create a strategic plan to help guide budget development and overall district priorities. It too engaged the public in the process, but in a different way. Rather than asking what programs, offerings, and types of staff the community felt were needed, district leaders asked questions about outcomes: What constitutes a successful education? What do you aspire for your children? How has the district made this happen? How has it failed in this pursuit?

What emerged was a reasonably clear vision of the outcomes desired by the community. It emphasized graduation from high school, the option for college, the skills for a career, and a safe, caring school environment. Happily, no laundry list of desired programs, purchases, or positions was generated because the community wasn't asked to do so. With these goals in mind, the district leadership looked internally and to the research to answer the question: What was needed to make this vision a reality? A deep dive into the data and best practices identified these changes as critical:

- More students must read on grade level.
- Fewer students must drop out.
- Some students needed a more personalized learning experience.

At this point, the school board and public were asked to bless the vision of success and the major focus areas. At this high level, broad-based buy-in was achieved.

If the district had stopped here, it's likely that little agreement on how to spend shrinking funds would have emerged. Just as a long detailed list of wants can provide justification for almost anything, a short vision statement also can provide cover for almost any spending. The district went one step further. It planned in detail how to bring about these three changes. There are many paths to this end, but through a series of facilitated planning sessions it created its particular plan, which included specifics like:

- *Reading at the elementary level.* Codify a districtwide approach to reading, develop common lessons, measure student growth monthly, and add instructional coaching.
- *Reading at the secondary level.* Provide credit-bearing reading instruction in middle and high school for all students below grade level.

And on the list went, but just for about a page and a half. As leaders, they agreed on a focused plan to address the key levers to achieve a vision set by the community.

Again, the school board was asked to bless this plan. Wisely, the plan was presented by a broad-based team of principals and central office administrators who strongly endorsed the new direction. Most importantly, the discussion took place during the summer, far removed from budget season. It was a discussion of strategy and specific action plans, not line items and dollars. With a strong endorsement from the school board and a growing level of shared vision, the leadership team then, and only then, created the financial plan to implement their strategic plan.

With a bit of a thud, the leadership team realized they needed more curriculum leaders, reading coaches, reading teachers at the middle and high school, a different type of guidance counselor, and a school within a school in their largest campuses. And all this had a price tag in the millions. It was daunting, but not overwhelming. If this is what we need, they reasoned, and no new dollars were available, other things must be cut to fund the district's new priorities.

They cut many existing expenses in these targeted areas, since they hadn't proved effective. They also cut many historic and peripheral programs, and they even bit the bullet and synchronized schedules at the secondary schools to share staff and reduce transportation costs, a move oft suggested but long resisted. So strong was the commitment to this clear, focused set of priorities that the special ed director offered to cut her own staffing to free up funds for high school reading teachers, and others made similar sacrifices without arm twisting or horse trading. The most striking test of commitment came when the state announced a multimillion-dollar further reduction in state aid in the midst of this budget planning. Rather than water down these new efforts, the team dug yet deeper into current spending. Like a well-trained basketball team with each player knowing where to go next on the court and how to support his teammates, the leadership team and the once-fractured school board passed sweeping budget changes year after year, despite shrinking revenue. A clear, thoughtful, strategic plan with a short list of concrete needs and unambiguous key programs, all grounded in a vision set by the community, made strategic budgeting possible despite an inhospitable context. In time, the district went on to win much national attention for raising reading scores and graduation rates.

3

ENGAGE AND ENLIST PRINCIPALS

*Principals Can Play an Outsized Role in
Creating Support for Tough Decisions*

When I first got involved in K–12 as a parent activist, I was surprised that so many people seemed against "progress." After years working in and with the central office, I have a much deeper appreciation for why some *oppose*, often strongly, a better use of limited dollars. I'm still surprised, however, by the limited number of people who *strongly* support the changes and provide an effective counterbalance to the opposition.

The scales often seem tipped toward those who oppose student-centered budgets. During budget season, if 200 people show up to a meeting, 190 are likely to be unhappy. Teachers, union officials, parents, students, former students, and parents of former students all come to the microphone to bury rather than praise.

Beyond outnumbering supporters nearly twenty to one, opponents also often bring more passion, volume, and commitment to their cause. Sometimes they chant, yell, cry, and plead. The few brave souls speaking in favor typically are calmer, quieter, and less frenetic. This lopsidedness makes it hard, even for reform-minded school boards, to pass unpopular budgets. The aftermath of such public budget "discussions" is often a watering down of the plans, a slower rollout, or outright abandonment of key improvement efforts, all in the name of being responsive to stakeholders and the public.

Driving home after many such meetings, I've wondered, why do so few speak on behalf of the kids in need? A good part of the reason is that school leaders—including principals—aren't included in the budgeting process in a meaningful way. When pushback occurs, they are often reluctant to speak out in favor of changes, even if they agree with them.

I was profoundly disappointed when a loud, ugly budget discussion followed such a path. I had proposed revamping our social and emotional support systems. The plan included expanding counseling through a cost-free partnership with a nonprofit agency and a university; providing high-quality, in-district substance abuse counseling through private insurance payments from students' families (the district would cover the uninsured and the provider waived the deductible in exchange for space in the schools); and providing high-level college counseling in partnership with outside experts.

For all the usual reasons, guidance counselors, social workers, and others opposed the changes. Staff were insulted by the outsiders; they argued these efforts were not needed, were wasteful, and so on. Hardly anyone spoke in favor of the effort. The silence was deafening, which was hard for me to understand, given recent history. In the prior two years, the district had suffered some real trauma. One student died while driving intoxicated, another took his own life, and the last few high school dances ended with an ambulance or two taking students to the

ER for alcohol poisoning—all this in recent memory, and yet nearly no one spoke up for the upgraded and expanded mental health counseling and drug addiction services.

The school board was waffling under the pushback and likely to not include these changes in the final budget. Frustrated and angry, I decided to meet with people who had privately supported the efforts. My first stop was the high school principal. He had been to the funerals with me. He called the parents of the kids in the ambulances.

My question for the principal was simple, "Why aren't you speaking out?" He assured me that he strongly supported the changes, that the services were desperately needed, and that the plan exceeded his wildest expectations in scope and quality. "We need this," he told me, and "I'm with you." At that moment, I felt better, but the feeling was fleeting: he then added, "You can't expect me to support this publicly."

Over the next decade and scores of budget battles in dozens of districts, I have come to see his actions as typical—not unusual or different at all from those of many (certainly not all) central office and building leaders. This is problematic in many ways:

- Principals have significant sway and clout with parents and teachers. Their support can bring parents on board and soften staff pushback.
- Principals know what's needed to implement new ideas well. Plans they help design are often better plans.
- Principals often water down the implementation of ideas they didn't champion.
- School boards are more likely to support a plan that has broad support from building leaders.

INCLUDE PRINCIPALS EARLY AND OFTEN

While I'm fearful of adding more to their already full plate, a bigger role for principals in creating the district budget would create more supporters for tough resource decisions. Principals, of course, already have a role in budgeting, but in many districts it's passive and often at odds with creating effective, student-centered budgets.

In the many hundreds of budget discussions in which I have participated, in a wide range of districts across the country, the most obvious observation is that the principals aren't in the room for most of these conversations. Central office folks lead the budget building effort. This is common in big districts and small ones alike. When principals *are* included in these deliberations, I'm taken aback that the superintendents often start the meeting by apologizing to them for taking them away from their schools. It seems like an apology is more appropriate if the district leadership planned how the district would spend its resources without the principals at the table. This is doubly true given that the lion's share of the budget funds school-based staff, materials, supplies, and curriculum.

It's not that principals are typically fully excluded from budgeting—just the opposite. They are usually involved, but not until after many of the big decisions are made. Budgets are often *shared* with principals but not *developed* with them. A mostly completed blueprint is offered for their feedback and support. They can try to tweak the plan, and maybe lobby to save or shift a position, but they seldom feel ownership of the budget given their limited input.

In one district the annual ritual of sharing the budget for input by principals was always tense. The building leaders sat around a long conference table, and a one-hundred-page document was handed to them. Successive central office leaders took turns reading aloud the major additions and subtractions in the proposal budget. As principals new to the district peppered questions at the administrators and hollered at the cuts, each presenter rebuffed them with well-worn phrases such as "We just can't afford that" or "We considered that" or the patronizing "I wish we could, but . . ." Veteran principals knew to sit back, hold their tongues, and just accept it.

This top-down central office approach has some pluses. It keeps principals focused on improving outcomes in their schools rather than in meetings reviewing dollars and cents. It doesn't ask leaders closest to the staff to make hard decisions about staffing (decisions many central office folks assume principals won't make), and it's a faster process because it involves fewer people and opinions, and certainly no one wants to stretch out budget building.

The minuses, however, are very detrimental to actually passing thoughtful, student-centered budgets. Beyond the direct value that principals offer as a good check and balance on creating practical strategies for raising achievement and knowing where some less effective dollars are being spent, their involvement can also lead to many more active supporters for the final budget.

Principals talk. They talk to teachers, parents, and school board members. What they say matters a great deal to a great many. When they mention that the new reading program in the proposed budget won't work because the coaches tasked with implementing it are underqualified, or that the cuts to nursing hours will lead to placing children in great danger and perhaps some might die, support fades fast.

On the flip side, imagine if the private whispers of principals instead suggested, "The new reading program is a moral imperative. It will change lives and we owe it to our children," and "I'm not worried about the changes to nursing hours because they are small. Many schools in the district have long used similar schedules, and be sure if I thought it was bad for kids I wouldn't let it happen in my school, but this is a reasonable plan."

Principals are key communicators in most districts, and what they say—often behind closed doors, in the hallways, or in the parking lot—makes or breaks support for a budget plan. The price of their support, however, is often providing them with a deep understanding of the district's and state's fiscal realities, actively involving them in setting priorities, and including their input in building comprehensive, coherent plans for raising achievement.

If you are thinking, "My district does include principals in budgeting and early in the process," then great. Be careful, however, that principal involvement isn't the "wish list" kind of involvement. Perhaps the only thing worse than not including principals in planning budgets is including and then ignoring them.

A fair many districts start their budget development process by asking principals what they "need" for next year. Templates or spreadsheets are provided, and principals are given a few weeks to submit their budget requests. Because there is often little up-front sharing of the fiscal constraints at this point, little current hard data on enrollment, and little clear agreement on a district theory of action or strategic priorities, this engagement exercise can breed cynicism and opposition. Lacking real-world constraints or a uniform focus, the principals include lots of additions and few subtractions or shifts. Worse, savvy principals ask for much, knowing it will be pared back later, and offer up unpopular cuts that they suspect will be restored.

Asking principals to build these preliminary budgets might be an attempt at inclusion, but when many of their wants and wishes aren't ultimately funded, it's easy for them to feel that the final budget plan presented to the school board isn't their plan, and thus they're not likely to support it privately.

The other counterproductive form of principal inclusion to be avoided is the forced show of solidarity. In some districts principals sit behind the superintendent or in the front row at school board meetings as the budget is shared publicly. Their presence is intended to indicate support. It also encourages teachers and parents to ask in the following days, "How can you support such a plan?" to which the principal inevitably responds, "It would have been better if . . ." or "They came up with the plan; I guess it's the best they could do," politely disavowing any ownership and support.

Beyond lack of engagement, there are other reasons principals (and thus their fans) don't support tough but good-for-kids resource shifts. They may not see the need for change, they may view the plan as not comprehensive and thus unlikely to be effective, or they may expect that "this too shall pass." In fact, there are lots of reasons why principals fail to strongly support bold shifts in spending:

- *Rooting for the wrong team.* Principals live in two worlds. It's like they hold dual citizenship. Patrick Lencioni, in *Five Dysfunctions of a Team* (Jossey-Bass), brilliantly explains that many people belong to multiple teams at work. A principal plays on the school team and the district team. Belonging to multiple teams is normal in complex organizations like school districts, and needn't lead to a lack of support for important but difficult district initiatives, but it often does.

    Lencioni explains that people can have only one "first team." A Bostonian who moves to Chicago can root for both the Red Sox and the White Sox, but when they play each other, he roots for his first team. When leaders are confronted with a "good for the district, but opposed by their staff" proposal, they must choose sides. Often, supporting their teachers' preference carries the day.

If principals are going to put the district team first, they will have to have real input and decision-making power in districtwide decisions, including the budget.

- *Hoping for a pain-free alternative.* In some cases, school leaders support—strongly support—the direction of a particular change, but have in the back of their mind that there must be a way to get the good new stuff without negatively impacting so many staff in their schools. They support the plan, in concept, but not the particulars of how it will be funded. *Can't we add the elementary reading teachers we need and avoid reducing paraprofessionals in my school? Just cut back on all that PD offered by the central office!*

Whether this is a rationalization or a sincere belief, many leaders don't lend their support because they believe that a pain-free (for them and their staff) funding option must be out there, but just hasn't been offered up yet. There is almost no limit to the extremes to which this thinking can go. One district, facing years of declining enrollment and a $60 million deficit, was considering closing schools since it had one extra seat for every ten students and very small class sizes. This meant fewer teachers. The plan also called for some expanded PD and curriculum development. Most principals actively lobbied against these budget-balancing moves. The school board, seeing much opposition and only the superintendent and her cabinet advocating for the change, refused to support the plan and postponed the budget vote.

Still facing a gaping budget deficit, the district assembled most of the building and central office leaders and essentially asked them how they would close the spending gap and prepare staff for the coming of the Common Core. They had no shortage of ideas. In fact, through facilitated discussions, they generated more than one hundred ideas. Quite satisfied, they believed their list would close the gap twice over. When the finance team actually calculated what each idea would generate in savings, all the excitement left the room. Fully a quarter of the ideas saved almost nothing—closer to $10,000 than $1,000,000. A large chunk violated state or federal law, and many weren't allowed by their collective bargaining agreement. All told, only a few million dollars of the sixty needed could come from the leadership-generated ideas. This isn't an indictment of the leaders, but testimony to their lack of understanding as to what things cost and what's possible.

It also explained why they didn't support the very tough proposed changes. They had (or so they thought) dozens of better, less painful ways to get to the same outcome.

- *Using a misaligned reward system.* One of the biggest contributors to building leaders staying on the sidelines during budget deliberations is that they are actually rewarded when they do. No, they don't get a bonus check or a trip to Hawaii, but if we define a reward as more good things happening than bad, then most principals are rewarded when they don't publicly and actively support the superintendent's aggressive shift in resources.

- *Principals who have smooth-running schools are highly valued in most districts.* Everyone getting along, a sense of collaboration, and cordiality are prized. The leader with upset staff, a steady flow of grievances, and an unpleasant climate is seldom thanked or promoted. By not taking a public stance supporting proposals that negatively impact the staff in their schools, principals are rewarded with calmer schools, which are in turn rewarded in many ways.

While lack of principal support is understandable, it's not acceptable if districts want to make the most of their limited resources. To pass smart budgets—spending plans that raise achievement and support students' other needs—active, sincere, impassioned support from principals is a must. These influential stakeholders must move from the sidelines onto the playing field, playing for the district team. Fortunately, there are many ways to engage and enlist principals.

Include Principals Early On in the Planning

Since their support is key in the end, it's best to include principals at the start. Including key stakeholders in the planning process is a well-known change management strategy, not likely new to many readers. Oddly, however, it is not always applied to principals and budget building.

Having watched many dozens of districts (big and small alike) plan their budgets, I've observed that most often the initial discussions, the heavy lifting, and the areas for additions or cuts are crafted by a small group of central office folks, mostly direct reports to the superintendent. Principals are brought in near the end to "hear" the budget, to ask questions, or perhaps to be given the opportunity to tweak the plan. Brought in late to the game, after most of the big decisions have been made, principals seldom offer strong support with this approach.

When principals help set the priorities for the district, not just their schools, and engage in the formative research to identify the district's needs, they are much more likely to understand, embrace, and advocate for bold budgets.

Provide Principals a Deep Understanding of District Finances

Many principals don't have a deep understanding of district finances, and thus may resent the hard choices they are being asked to make and support. In some districts, there is a sense that central office should find the money for the schools and, worse, that a bloated central office robs schools of needed funds. These perceptions, even if untrue, can keep principals from supporting tough, student-centric budget decisions.

Even though the typical budget building cycle usually starts with a review of the district's overall financial picture—such as "enrollment is down 1.2 percent," "revenue will be up by 2.1 percent, expenses up by 4.3 percent," "the ABC grant is ending, so five positions must move back to the operating budget," and so on—too many times I have observed the lack of principal understanding of the district's financial position and the extent this undermines their support, both publicly and privately.

In one district, the financial woes seemed so large and public that it was easy to assume everyone knew the context. A high spending, affluent district got hit hard by a combination of a newly enacted state tax cap limiting spending increases to 2 percent a year, while benefit costs were rising fast and enrollment was shrinking. Historical increases averaged more than 6 percent a year. The math seemed simple and obvious:

the district needed 6 percent to keep up with costs and would get about 2 percent. Cuts were unavoidable. The budget plan was quite good, all things considered. It included two new efforts to improve student learning and an expansion of nonacademic offerings, and balanced the budget through attrition. It seemed like easy sailing. Wrong.

Principals pushed back aggressively; refused to support changes that would worsen staff reductions even if it meant more staff in other areas, which scuttled the improvements; and riled up the parents and staff. Most surprisingly, they offered no alternative, not even the ever-popular "cut central office" cure-all. In the end, no new initiatives were approved, and across-the-board cuts prevailed.

During the postmortem, the district uncovered some of the underlying causes of the pushback from these key, should-have-been-advocate principals:

- They believed the tax cap "wasn't real." Why? Because in the first year of the cap, no cuts were made. They didn't know that the district drained its reserve funds to maintain a 6 percent increase for one more year, and that the fund was now depleted.
- They thought shrinking enrollment meant lower costs, such as the need to buy fewer textbooks. That meant savings could be found elsewhere to make up for the cuts. They didn't realize that textbooks were a few hundred dollars a student, but reduced per-pupil state aid due to shrinking enrollment meant the continual loss of many *thousands* of dollars per student.
- They believed that since employees took a "pay cut" in the last negotiations, the budget should be flush. The payout was actually an increase, but smaller than in the past.

- They saw health insurance costs were dropping, and assumed this freed up funds. The reality was the district was paying more per employee, but so were employees, who assumed as they paid more for insurance the district paid less.

With this misunderstanding of financial realities, it's no surprise they resisted the cuts.

Contrast this to another district that spent weeks teaching the principals the ins and outs of school finance. First, town finance officials explained the sources and uses of funds over four hours of presentations to district and building leaders. Principal comments after the presentations showed how valuable the time spent was. "I had no idea that schools were the largest expenditure in town," and "Are you telling me, every year for the last few, the town has gone into debt to fund our operating budgets?" Yes! How did this happen, they asked. Changes in state aid formulas caused a dramatic drop in funding. As a follow-on, a two-hour presentation by an outside health insurance consultant explained how costs to the district had risen in recent years even as employee contributions, copays, and deductibles increased.

In both cases, the presenters were known to be sympathetic to the school and school spending. This is key. Sometimes, antitax, fiscal conservatives offer to give these talks, but principals stop listening after "Good morning."

At the announcement of this lecture series, the principals balked at being out of their buildings for money talk; it seemed wrong to them. By the end they all shared that they never knew why money was so tight.

It is critical to let the audience ask questions and provide detailed answers. Each speaker came back at least twice, allowing time for questions to bubble up.

"Couldn't the town just raise taxes?" Yes, but it requires town meeting approval and the district promised no tax increase for five years in exchange for the last increase.

"Couldn't we just raise trash collection fees?" The projections already include the fee increase you heard about in the paper. "Oh, that's worse than I thought," shared one surprised principal.

FORCE PRINCIPALS TO WRESTLE WITH THE TRADE-OFFS

Understanding that times are tight is a key first step to winning the ever-important support of principals, but it's not enough. Often, they still struggle to understand the scope of the need. A reaction like "If times are tough, I can give up my secretary for the summer," while heartfelt and sincere, won't close a $3,000,000 budget gap.

A simple Excel spreadsheet or paper worksheet can go a long way in helping principals grasp the size of shifts needed and build support for the student-centric changes. The sheet has three sections that help answer three questions:

1. How big is the budget gap?
2. What new spending is needed to improve outcomes?
3. What possibilities are under consideration to shift funds?

The first section should be uncontroversial if the principals have a deep understanding of the financial context of the district, city/town, and state.

The second section surprises some. Including new efforts, despite tight budgets, also helps build principal support. At first, principals might balk at having to cut deeper to fund new efforts, especially so when "central office" is doing the cutting and their schools are getting the cuts, but when they are guiding the *spending* it's much more energizing and easier to think the budget is a force for good, not just a chore to be balanced. How can we add new staff while we are cutting? Since tight budgets aren't a short-term problem, districts can't just wait for the good old days to return before funding new and improved efforts. In some cases principals see budget balancing as not their job, but rather the purview of the superintendent and school board. Balancing the budget, providing less for kids, and angering staff aren't typically at the top of their "can't wait to do" list. Fighting for better services and outcomes for their students, however, does fit squarely into their view of their job. When additions are combined with the subtractions, it's easier for principals to engage in a passionate manner.

The sum of sections one and two equal what needs to be cut, shifted, or raised. It's the total funding gap. Section three should list all the reasonable possibilities for raising revenue, ending programs, cutting expenses, or repurposing existing staff or dollars. Box 3.1 offers some helpful resources to augment this spreadsheet.

Each option in section three should not be a fixed amount, but rather a variable depending on scale with the savings automatically recalculated in real time. For example, rather than have the option to increase class size in honors classes by two students and save $50,000 or increase lunch prices by 10 cents and raise $75,000, the options should be to increase average honors class by x students and increase lunch by y cents. Making the scope of changes a variable turns the option from a "yes or no" question into a "how much" question.

Every option on the list should be an okay option. All the choices must be consistent with the strategic plan, theory of

BOX 3.1

GOOD OPTIONS FOR
DOING MORE WITH LESS

Creating the choices for what's doable and reasonable to free up funds is no simple task, but an ever-growing body of research and practical advice is available. Useful resources include:

- Nathan Levenson, *Smarter Budgets, Smarter Schools* (Cambridge, MA: Harvard Education Press, 2012).
- Nathan Levenson, Karla Baehr, James C. Smith, and Claire Sullivan, *Spending Money Wisely: Getting the Most from School District Budgets* (Boston: District Management Council, 2014), www.dmcouncil.org.
- "Smarter School Spending for Student Success," www.smarterschoolspending.org/.

action, and core values. The district should be able to live with any combination from the list.

When I first tried this three-step process as a superintendent with a group of principals and department leaders they pushed back, saying it was too hard and not their job. They also wanted more choices than what I had listed in the third section of the paper form, since they didn't like any of the options provided. Giving them the opportunity to add to the list helped bring them further on board. With the expanded list and the form transferred to Excel to provide each person the chance to vary the scale of each potential change, the principals individually wrestled with the options on their laptops. Nearly all at first set the variables low—raise honors classes by half a student on average; raise lunch by a nickel. After about thirty minutes they declared victory. They had made their choices. Only one problem: none had closed more than 25 percent of the budget gap. I ended the session with a warning. We would meet every week until we created a plan that was supported by a majority of the cabinet, closed 100 percent of the budget gap, and funded all of the new strategic priorities.

After four more planning sessions, a thoughtful, balanced budget emerged. It funded the strategic initiatives, such as reading coaches and a data analyst, but some of the near-consensus recommendations surprised even the principals themselves. Initially every elementary principal opted not to increase lunch prices. But as the principals played with the tool, they realized that every dime added to lunch saved a teacher. The impact surprised them, in the same way they were surprised how little was saved for each week school secretaries didn't work in the summer. One less week for all summer admins didn't even save $10,000. This prompted good questions: "What do other like-districts charge for lunch?" (Fifty to seventy cents more.) "Does the lunch program turn a profit?" (No, it runs at a loss.) "When did lunch prices go up last?" (Many years ago.) In the end, they opted to raise lunch prices by fifty cents.

The power of their participation became evident a few weeks later. After we presented the jointly developed budget, parents started calling school board members to complain about the lunch increases. PTO presidents raced to meet with the principals, and teachers fretted that some kids would go hungry. This had all the makings of a fast retreat by the school board and nonstrategic across-the-board cuts, a favorite peace-making strategy for the district. It would also likely pare back the reading and the data initiative.

Without being asked, the principals sprang into action. They assured their teachers that district policy guaranteed no student would be denied lunch for financial reasons, and they would ensure this never happened in their school. The teachers trusted these assurances from their principal. An identical pledge from the superintendent wouldn't have been as convincing. The principals also artfully worked with the parent groups. "Do you know," they explained, "about the town's structural deficit? Do you know that we charge less for lunch than other districts, and even with this increase we are near the bottom of like communities? Did you know that the lunch program doesn't cover its costs, and most importantly, that if we don't do this, the school will lose a reading teacher?"

No, the parents hadn't known any of this. One PTO president sputtered, "I can't believe you are supporting this decision." The principal responded that she too was surprised, but it was the best decision given the needs of our students and fiscal realities: "I don't like it, but it's better than anything else." The pushback subsided fairly quickly, and the budget passed as designed.

Provide Principals Time to Think and Get Comfortable

Beyond simply offering principal participation, the process also provided the gift of time. Multiple hard meetings doesn't feel like a gift at first, but leaders need lots of time to understand the context, to wrestle with the trade-offs, to ask questions, and then to process the answers. Participatory budget planning can require meeting every week for a few hours for about ten weeks before the first submission of a budget to the school board. Some will feel the focus should be more on teaching and learning, but funding teaching and learning priorities *is* focusing on teaching and learning.

I learned that some of the principals in my district had shared our budgeting process with a job alike group. Principals from twenty other districts were dumbstruck that they actually had a meaningful say in the budgeting process. "You're so lucky," one commented. "Lucky?" replied a principal from my district, "I never thought of myself as lucky, having to make such ugly decisions, but I guess you're right. Much better to have a voice than just be left out and complain."

It wasn't all Kumbaya, however. We had to implement a few ground rules to preserve civility and openness, such as elementary principals had to make cuts or exchanges mostly at the elementary level, not primarily at the secondary, and vice versa. There was a tendency to try to shift the pain to others.

Change the Incentives by Prioritizing Improved Student Achievement

I have wondered a lot why so many principals and other administrators hang back or opt to protect their staff rather than support student-centric budgets. I'm reminded of philosopher Edmund Burke's comment, "The only thing necessary for the triumph of evil is for good men to do nothing." Applied to schools, I think the only thing necessary for the triumph of the status quo is for good principals to do nothing. Unfortunately, in many districts a smart administrator realizes, as mentioned previously, that there are rewards for supporting the staff in the building and few drawbacks to not pushing for tough, painful decisions.

Imagine the principal of the Kennedy School—smart, caring, well organized, and very popular with parents and staff alike. He greets students every morning, knows all their names on the first day, calls parents back quickly, helps teachers in need, and has built a collaborative atmosphere in the school, with little staff turnover and hardly a complaint. He is often mentioned as a potential assistant superintendent if we can pry him from his school.

Across town, at the King School, it's a very different story. The principal, equally smart and caring, is known to lack good people skills. Some staff are very unhappy and share their unhappiness with school board members on a regular basis. The social climate is not overly pleasant. The PTO is concerned that the teachers are concerned, and there are whispers as to whether the principal's contract will be renewed.

This is a true story (school names have been changed), but an incomplete one. The students at the very happy Kennedy School achieve well below their demographically similar peers in the district and state. They have for years, and the trajectory is flat to negative. The children in the less-than-cheery King School had also been underperforming, but have seen significant growth in test scores in the last few years—growth made possible by some big and tough realignment of resources supported by the principal, including fewer paraprofessionals, more reading teachers, and slightly larger class size in exchange for increased social and emotional supports. In short, the principal rocked the boat and shifted resources, and kids learned more despite shrinking budgets. She also worried her job was in jeopardy and her reputation was sullied, and her spirits dropped.

Keeping the peace, being friendly (which often includes not giving hard feedback to teachers), and running a smooth operation is highly prized and very visible. When visiting schools across the country, after I'm introduced by a superintendent to a great principal, I make it a point to ask in private, how does student achievement and academic growth in the great principal's school compare to like students? "I'm not sure" is the most common response. Some go so far as to ask why I'm asking, not seeing my less-than-subtle poke at their praise for their colleagues.

Certainly, the kind words by the superintendent could just be polite small talk, like politicians extolling the beauty of just of every baby they see. To push my point, I have asked superintendents to tell me who their top principals are and which are closer to the bottom. Few hesitate; they have their lists. The follow-up question, "Why are they strong?" generally includes how well their school is run, the good relationships they have with staff, and perhaps some innovative programs they have implemented. Seldom is increasing student achievement from x to y mentioned as proof of excellence.

Some districts that have a much easier time moving funds around, and strong support from principals for such moves, have much more explicit rewards (and negative consequences) based on student achievement results. When I speak with building leaders in these settings, I am struck by how differently they approach hard budget decisions. To be clear, they don't care more for children, don't have higher ideals or aspirations, are not smarter or harder working. What differentiates them is they find different balance points between their conflicting desires to help students and minimize any negative impact on staff.

These principals felt more pressure to raise achievement. They weren't skittish people constantly looking over their shoulder, worried the axe would drop any minute, but they did mention, unprompted, that "If we don't raise achievement, I won't be a principal for a long time in this district," or "We are a 'needs improvement' district, and the state may step in if we don't continue the growth," or "I want to move up and no one moves up without showing results."

In all these instances, they felt there was a downside for them personally and professionally, real and tangible, if students didn't learn and results didn't improve. They could usually point to at least a few people who had been asked to leave based on lackluster results. This worry seemed to counterbalance their equally strong desire to be good to their staff and build a supportive, welcoming culture. They didn't let the results focus turn them into mean, tough bosses, but it did make them much more comfortable stopping what wasn't working and shifting staff and funds. They knew a good culture and good morale were important, but they didn't think they were sufficient and should trump all else.

RECRUIT AND HIRE PRINCIPALS WHO WILL MAKE TOUGH RESOURCE DECISIONS

Rewarding academic achievement can make principals (and others) better managers of resources, but it doesn't always. In every one of these outcomes-focused districts I've met plenty of school leaders who shied away from tough budget decisions. The second factor at play is that these results-focused districts tend to attract a greater number of results-focused principals. Regardless of any external pressures, many principals were internally pushing themselves for better, measurable academic results and had much greater comfort with shifting resources and staff in the process. They wanted happy staff and worked hard to ease any pain, but more naturally supported tough decisions just the same.

So how does a district find such principals? What skills should one look for in principal candidates in districts wanting leaders with strong budgeting skills and wanting to ensure resources are allocated wisely? It might seem logical that in an era of declining resources, financially savvy school leaders would be in demand. Former CPAs, business-to-education career changers, and people good with numbers or strong Excel skills come to mind. Unfortunately, this doesn't get at the crux of the challenge. Such a solution implies that the problem is that some leaders don't know how to manage a budget and more technical expertise will help.

Nearly every current school leader I know already has ideas for what spending to stop, what to add, and what to shift in order to raise achievement. The underlying limitation isn't knowledge as much as it is willingness.

Some districts, and many private sector organizations, use tools during the interview process to screen for desirable traits. Myers Briggs, Caliper, DISC, and other self-administered personality profile tools can gauge whether a candidate has a greater need to be liked, tries to avoid conflicts, values process versus an internal focus on results, is comfortable with hard decisions, or wants to see the most benefit from every dollar, hour, or person. For internal candidates, such as teachers looking to become assistant principals, or assistant principals wanting to become principals, some districts have included likely candidates in the budgeting development process to observe their willingness to make tough decisions.

The connection between human capital decisions and practices and spending money smartly is real, and perhaps too often overlooked. While there is not a definitive test that will determine if a candidate for a principalship (or central office role) will be have a predilection for spending limited dollars wisely, there are a number of tools that can provide predictive insights. Using personality and value assessments in the hiring process might seem very unorthodox, but it is a well-established practice outside of K–12. In fact, such tests are used to assess the personality, skills, cognitive abilities, and other traits of 60–70 percent of prospective workers in the United States, up from 30–40 percent about five years ago.[1]

The CALIPER pre-employment profile is popular in the private sector and widely used in knowledge-based business. This assessment and related interpretation by skilled specialists can benchmark potential new leaders on a wide range of traits, a number of which are valuable for making and advocating for tough, student-first budget decisions.

Fortunately, these same resource-related traits are also very beneficial for seeking instructional leaders, especially if you're looking for change agents. These nationally normed assessments can gauge the level of a person's desire to accommodate others' needs, willingness to push forcefully, cautiousness, comfort at handling rejection and criticism, and so on. A high need to please others and a low threshold for criticism, for example, can be a recipe for avoiding making budget shifts that would make staff unhappy.

The Myers Briggs Personality Type is more common in public schools. This well-established tool has many supporters and critics alike in K–12. While no assessment is perfect and all of us are more complicated than any of the sixteen personality types in the Myers Briggs universe, the tool has helped me screen for leaders who are much more willing to make tough, student-centered budget decisions.

Myers Briggs classifies people along four dimensions, two of which are very insightful: how people gather information (Sensing versus Intuition, or S and N in Myers Briggs–speak) and how people make decisions (Thinking versus Feeling, or T and F) explain a lot.

Those who are predominantly Sensing (S) look for very specific facts and concrete details, and therefore get less excited by abstract concepts such as aligning resources to priorities and investing in the new and unseen at the expense of the here and now. The lack of fine-grained details about the new plans also makes them nervous. Intuition (N)-leaning leaders are comfortable thinking about the future, are comfortable with conceptually based changes, and don't need or even want all the details worked out in advance of making the decision.

The Thinking versus Feeling axis explains a lot when the resource decisions involve reducing staff. Those who score high on Thinking (T) are much more comfortable with the cuts ("if that's what the numbers suggest would be best"), whereas others place much more weight on the need to protect staff. Both types care a lot about teachers and students, but how they reconcile these conflicting values differs greatly.

One pioneer in applying personality profiles to K–12, Lyle Kirtman, has worked with over three hundred school districts in helping recruit and hire principals, central office leaders, and superintendents. After profiling over six hundred administrators and tracking their actions and performance on the job, he found some strong patterns. On the whole, ENTJ types make effective school and district leaders who will also make the tough, student-centered budget decisions.[2] Their profile is as follows:

- *Extroverted (E)*: A strong communicator who builds a network of support
- *Intuitive (N)*: A strategic thinker who tends to look for root causes for problems
- *Thinking (T)*: An objective and analytical thinker
- *Judging (J)*: A leader who can develop and execute a plan of action with a focus on results

Lots of caveats abound. Some people reject outright Myers Briggs, while others argue it is best used as just one of many factors and better yet when test results are evaluated by a skilled analyst. Moreover, ENTJ isn't right for every culture or context.

These people tend to be highly directive, which may not be best for every situation. Most importantly, not every good educational leader or budgeter is an ENTJ.

The other personality assessment that can be helpful is the Personal Inventory of Attitudes and Values (PIAV). This tool helps surface a person's belief system along six dimensions, including a few that have significant bearing on a leader's willingness to move resources and support these decisions. The three most relevant dimensions to managing resources are:

1. *Traditional.* Scoring high indicates a desire to maintain past practices. A lower score is someone who's more comfortable with change.
2. *Social.* Scoring high indicates a strong appreciation of people and their feelings. A lower score indicates someone more likely to make a decision that negatively impacts colleagues and staff.
3. *Utilitarian.* A high score indicates a comfort with things financial and a desire to make every dollar useful. A low score indicates someone who isn't wasteful, but just isn't as moved by "bang for the buck" analysis.

Do Empowered Principals Make Better Resource Decisions?

All this talk of the importance of principals in developing and advocating for wise budgets raises the question: Should principals actually be in charge of school budgets, not just at the table helping to craft them? In central offices and school board meetings across the country the phrase "principal empowerment" or "school-based budgeting" seems to be uttered with greater frequency and much optimism. The strategy of empowering principals is gaining popularity in large urban districts, turnaround schools, and many suburban districts. A common theme is that principals are closer to the children, better understand their needs, and can make more thoughtful and targeted decisions than the more distant (and perhaps political and bureaucratic) central office.

Empowering a principal usually includes granting the authority to make some or all of the following decisions:

- How dollars are spent in the school
- Which types of roles or positions are staffed in the school
- What materials and curriculum are used in the school
- Who works in the school

Three of these four empowerments are budget-related, so principal empowerment is, in part, a strategy to shift how resource decisions are made. So do empowered principals make good budget decisions? From my work and research, I believe the answer is yes under the right conditions, and no otherwise.

Simply handing the budget reins over to principals doesn't erase all the pressures to please staff and parents, to avoid ugly confrontations, and to address the multitude of other pressures that make smarter budgets so unpopular and hard to pass. In fact, principals are closer to their staff, as well as their students, and thus may be even more reluctant than central office to make hard decisions impacting teachers. In one district that empowered its principals the most common spending changes were the addition of more assistant principals and reduction in class size. Neither strategy raised achievement (nor does the research suggest that it should).

So what are the right conditions in which empowered principals make better resource decisions? The first is a high level of accountability. Since there is always pressure from within the school against hard budget choices, there needs to be even greater pressure from outside to encourage tough decisions. In districts like Jefferson Parish (just outside New Orleans) and New York City, empowered principals, who have wide-ranging authority on how dollars are spent and on whom they are spent, did make big gains and shifted resources in the process. New York won the Broad Prize in 2007 for most improved urban district, and Jefferson Parish increased the percentage of students performing at basic or above levels by nine percentage points in five years from 2009 to 2013, while the state improved at approximately half that rate. As a result the district's state accountability score increased to a B grade from a D grade, more than doubling the number of students in the district attending higher rated schools.[3]

Both district gains were, in large part, through pairing accountability and empowerment. The big gains accompanied significant accountability—not just measuring and reporting achievement results (which is perhaps "accountability light"), but rather the large-scale replacement of principals who didn't get results. In both districts it was commonplace for empowered principals to be removed if results didn't improve. Yes, time and help were given, but it was normal and expected that ineffective leaders couldn't stay. In our interviews, these principals talked openly about their greater willingness to shift staff and resources because they couldn't risk continuing with ineffective programs, strategies, or people.

The other key precondition for empowered principals to make better budget decisions is to actually give the principals the authority to make better budget decisions. This seems obvious, but in a recent survey conducted by the District Management Council of district-identified "empowered principals," most actually had very little actual budget authority. This included turnaround schools that had, in theory, statutory or legislatively granted extra autonomy. In many cases district class size caps limited greatly how many teachers they could hire, and more often than not the empowered principals couldn't exchange types of staff, such as a librarian for a reading teacher, or a school psychologist for a social worker, or a classroom teacher for an instructional coach.

Perhaps the biggest obstacle to actually empowering principals, especially in districts where only some schools had extra autonomy, was central office not getting the memo. In many of the districts, the principal was handed budget authority over "school-based staff," but many of the adults in the building were classified as "district-based," such as special education teachers, school psychologists, ELL teachers, and instructional coaches. These principals had no say over how many of these people worked in their school or what they did.

Accountability and actual authority are structural prerequisites for empowering principals, but there are more subtle requirements as well: skill and will. It's common for principals to gripe about central office, but when handed the reins, many quickly discover that it's hard and not much fun to manage the budget. More than a few have confided in me that they are uncomfortable with the power and confused by the finances. Just as not every principal is ready to be an instructional leader, not every instructional leader is ready to effectively manage school budgets.

In the right situation, with reasonable accountability and in the hands of a skilled and thoughtful leader, an empowered principal can be a wise and effective budget builder, but it is no easy task to get all the puzzle pieces to fit together.

4

TAKE STEPS TO MINIMIZE THE PAIN

*With Tight Resources, Many Budgets Include
Some Pain, but There Are Many Ways to Reduce
the Hurt and Still Fund What Matters Most*

Passing smarter budgets almost always includes a dose of pain and suffering for some staff. This is very unfortunate and hard to avoid. Since people make up roughly 80 percent of a typical school district budget, as costs and needs rise faster than revenues, which is the case in most districts these days, one of two realities exists:

1. future budgets will fund fewer people; or
2. some people will be paid less than in the past.

Absent more funds, one or both must be true. For many districts, a combination of both lies ahead. This reality creates an enormous barrier to passing student-centered budgets. This challenge is magnified because few districts would be pleased to just hold on to what they have and do today. Higher standards and more challenging students call for new programs or new strategies. These new strategies for helping students often require reductions to make way for the new.

No one wants to see anyone lose their job. So it's natural that the staff, community, and school boards are reluctant to reduce staffing, even when the budget can't afford to keep everyone. In many school districts, however, the reasonable desire to minimize the negative impact on teachers, paraprofessionals, and administrators has unintentionally slowed efforts to raise achievement, graduation rates, and college and career readiness. Passing smarter budgets requires district leaders to thoughtfully balance the needs of students and the adults who educate them.

Minimizing tight budgets' negative impact on staff is a good thing. Hardworking, dedicated people who are devoted to helping students deserve to be treated well. Helping kids without negatively impacting staff was easier when new dollars funded new efforts; the new staff didn't displace the old programs or people. This approach certainly makes it easier to roll out new efforts, but it's important to keep in mind that this approach isn't actually good, it's just easier. This avoidance of pain often leads to layering new efforts on top of old ones, maintains ineffective efforts, and splinters central office support, all to the detriment of students.

The desire to protect staff from budget cuts runs deep in school districts. One district I worked with, for example, identified a significant challenge facing some high school students. This high performing system had much success at the Advanced Placement level, with lots of kids going to the Ivy League, yet roughly 25 percent of its students struggled mightily in English and math. A deep dive into the issue revealed that many of these struggling students were taught math and English from special education teachers and tutors, who had little to no mastery of the material themselves. The low student achievement was clearly linked to staff being asked to teach, reteach, and preteach complex content like Algebra II that they themselves struggled with. The district, with energy and determination, set out to add more math and English teachers at the high school to help these students. In the end, it did find the dollars for these content-strong teachers, but it also kept the original teachers and tutors. Students got extra help from the new staff and also from the original team. None of the district leaders thought the second extra help period was needed, few thought it helped, and some lamented that students gave up an elective to make room for it in their schedules. So why did they layer on, rather than add by subtraction? Because they had the funds to do it all and felt it wasn't fair to the original staff to cut their positions since they hadn't done anything wrong, even if the money and time could have been put to better use.

Minimizing negative impact on current staff is both caring and necessary to win support and reduce pushback for student-centered shifts in the budget. Leaders needn't fear the pushback, but rather should take proactive steps to reduce it. The first step in managing pushback is to understand its many causes. Staff can be negatively impacted from budget changes in three ways, and each dictates a different strategy to overcome it:

1. Job loss
2. Income loss
3. Diminished self-esteem

OVERCOMING SELF-CENSORSHIP

Trying to avoid losing one's job is a very real and reasonable cause of resistance to shifting funds around in the budget. A budget proposal that calls for cutting positions has obvious and significant negative impact on those who lose their jobs. Good people, understandably, don't feel good about causing someone to become unemployed. It is the hardest part of leadership—so hard that many school and district leaders self-censor these decisions. Self-censorship runs strong in many leadership teams.

I have worked with many district leadership teams to help them understand and then overcome self-censorship. The exercise, a thought experiment, is called Moving to the Moon. It goes as follows.

Earth has recently colonized the moon and has just completed construction of an exact replica of all of your district school buildings, as well as added a dome to hold in an atmosphere and a big machine that creates Earth-like gravity. Your district has won the lottery and 100 percent of your students and families will be relocating lunar-side next year.

Since we are starting from scratch, the first question is: What programs, practices, and policies would you take to the moon and which would you leave behind? I have facilitated this exercise with districts both big and small. Very animated discussion usually takes place. Often, the schools on the moon would have a stronger emphasis on reading, more time for the arts, fewer special ed classes, more response to intervention (RTI), fewer paraprofessionals . . . and on the list goes. One takeaway is that building and district leaders aren't short on ideas to improve their schools, and there's plenty they would leave behind.

At this point I share that while all the students have seats on the rocket ferry, none of the teachers, paras, or assistant principals have tickets. They can hire a whole new staff if they wish. They are asked what might be different about the mix of people, skills, and roles—a relatively easy question for most to answer. Then another wrinkle is added. Building schools on the moon, they learn, is expensive, so we will have slightly less money per pupil, and as they make their staffing plan for their far-off district, they will need to trim some positions. At this point, different teams tend to veer in one of two directions. Some say, "New planet, same old headaches," and focus on the impossible and unreasonable nature of the task. They don't like the thought experiment. Others, however, keep moving forward, sometimes with great excitement.

Some have no trouble fleshing out their new dream team. They typically bring many of their current team, but seldom everyone. For me, the interesting part isn't the details of their plan, but rather how detailed their plans are. In many districts, leaders have a clear picture of what staffing plan is best for their students and costs less, and it's often quite different from what they have in their Earth-side schools.

At this point the last question is thrown to the group: Why don't we adopt this moon-based plan here on Earth, through the next budget? Usually, all the energy leaves the room. Awkward silence or comments like "It's not that easy" and "It wouldn't be fair" fill the void. Follow-on conversations often clarify the issue as "Yes, if we were starting from scratch we would staff and spend differently, but it's unfair, unethical, or undoable to do it differently when everything (everyone) is already in place."

Mind games aren't the only place we see lots of self-censorship; it plays out regularly as districts work to raise achievement. The challenge to ensure all students read well by the end of grade 3 is a striking case in point that hits at the intersection of teaching and learning and self-censorship. There are few topics in

K–12 that have broader, more passionate agreement than the importance of elementary reading.

One district I worked with recently, for example, researched the background and skills of every person providing extra help to struggling readers, and concluded that nearly none had the skills, training, or background to be effective at the task. As internal budget deliberations rolled around, I expected they would recommend shifting spending significantly away from paraprofessionals and tutors to certified reading teachers. Unfortunately, this wasn't the case. As the debate shifted from concept ("We need highly skilled teachers") to specifics ("How many reading paras will be replaced in each school?"), everything changed.

Rather than focusing on the limited and inadequate training and skills of the paraprofessionals, district leaders talked about how long the paras had worked in the district, how Mary befriended a student a few years ago, and how much the paras liked being part of the school community. At the end of the day, the paras stayed and struggling readers continued to struggle.

Self-censorship is not a sign of a weak leader, just an experienced one. It only takes witnessing one packed and angry school board meeting, one vote of no confidence by the union, or a school board failing to approve tough cuts for a district or school leader to make you shy away from proposing cutting positions, especially beloved positions.

A year later, surprisingly, the district (the very same leaders) did reduce paraprofessional staffing by a third and hired skilled reading teachers as part of an aggressive effort to improve reading by utilizing many of the ideas that follow.

Self-censorship won't easily go away, but if we minimize the negative impact on staff, there can be less need for it.

Attrition Helps Smooth the Way

Fortunately, there are ways to help students and be fair to staff. The most effective strategy is the "attrition" strategy. I remember a phone call from the superintendent of a small district who joyfully announced that five special education teachers were leaving—two were retiring, two moving out of state, and one choosing to stay home with her children. The superintendent's glee wasn't because he disliked or didn't value these teachers, but he did want five fewer special education teachers as part of a strategy to add math and English teachers to serve some students with IEPs. These five resignations made his plan possible.

Obviously there would be no pushback to the change in staffing because these five teachers wanted to leave! Had all the special education staff chosen to return, it's likely that the proposed budget would have included, at most, one new math or English teacher. My guess, however, is that self-censorship would have led the district to maintain the status quo entirely.

Many superintendents already use attrition to help ease budget changes, but the approach can be fine-tuned and expanded. To start, it's helpful to quantify the potential opportunity to shift staffing based on attrition. It's rare when I ask "What's the historic attrition rate of the speech therapists or paraprofessionals?" that anyone around the budget table can answer the question beyond "not much" or "some, most years."

Attrition rates vary greatly by district and role, but are fairly steady within a particular role and district. In some places 10 percent of special education teachers or elementary classroom teachers voluntarily leave each year, but far fewer middle school or PE teachers don't return. No budget deliberation should begin without data on staff attrition by role and level.

By looking at three years of data, district leaders can identify trends and make reasonable forecasts. It's surprising how much latitude attrition can provide for layoff-free staff reductions. For many roles, attrition of 3 to 5 percent a year is common. Even at the low end, over three years, nearly one out of every ten FTE in a given role or department could be reduced and dollars shifted with no one being pushed out of their job.

Attrition is, however, often underutilized because in most districts, budget calendars and HR calendars are out of sync. Budgets are built in January or February, and staff notify the district they are not returning in May, June, or even August. This makes it hard and risky to incorporate attrition into budget planning for lack of certainty that someone will leave. Here are a few options to help take full advantage of normal staff turnover:

- *Offer incentives for early notification.* Offer a cash bonus for staff informing the district early that they are not returning—say $2,000 if they notify by February 1. This has the ancillary benefit of the district being able to recruit new staff much sooner, which helps raise the quality of the candidate pool.

- *Make contingent decisions.* When the goal is to shift resources, rather than definitively cutting a line item, districts can set the direction during the winter budget planning phase but not the exact pace. One district's budget included provisions that additional reading teachers would be hired to the extent that tutors and custodians chose not to return. Yes, the district would have liked to hire ten new reading teachers, and yes, it believed the Title I tutors weren't the best choice for teaching reading, and yes, benchmarking had indicated it had more custodians than needed, but if-then budgeting eliminated much of the anguish from such cuts. In two years the district got its ten reading teachers, and no one in the district lost their job involuntarily.

- *Hedge your bets.* If annual attrition for a given role has averaged 6 percent a year, and never dropped below five FTE in recent years, then planning on four layoff-free reductions may be a reasonable decision during budget planning.
- *Conduct unofficial surveys.* There are many reasons that staff don't disclose their intention to leave or retire. Some want to keep all options open, others fear becoming less influential, and a few just don't see any reason to come forward before the official notification date, which is often well after the budget is passed. An unofficial, nonbinding survey can provide confidence for budget planners opting to hedge shifts based on attrition.

Attrition can be a strategic budgeter's friend, but it can also be a siren luring you to crash on the rocks if taken to extremes. One district, for example, knew that it had more high school teachers than required, given declining enrollment. It decided to trim through attrition. When two Spanish teachers left, Spanish class sizes increased to unreasonable levels but other departments remained untouched. When two math teachers left, English was spared a cut even though enrollment drops hit both departments equally.

Transfers to Other Openings

Attrition can provide pain-free maneuvering room for roles with lots of staff, but for roles with just a few people or even one person, past trends don't help. Rather than counting on attrition, adopting a "soft landing" strategy can help reduce pushback from eliminating positions. Losing one's job is very harsh and often generates strong sympathetic pushback. Plans that provide a *different* job for those impacted by budget cuts and changes can help reduce opposition.

As part of consolidating a few roles into a unified STEM (science, technology, engineering, and mathematics) leadership position, one district shifted a central office math director into a high school AP math teacher and instructional coach, ensuring her a job. The director still wasn't happy, but it dramatically reduced pushback from others. "At least she still has a job in the district," murmured many.

WHEN JOB LOSS CAN'T BE AVOIDED

No one wants to see anyone lose their job, but reductions in force are a common reality in K–12. Having watched or helped many districts through this process, I have noticed that fairness is a critical ingredient in winning support for these tough decisions. Let's take a crazy example to make a point. If a district announced that to balance the budget all left-handed staff shorter than 5'4" would be cut, no one would support such a decision. Beyond its lack of strategic focus, it's just not fair! While this may seem obvious, the intriguing twist is how the definition of fairness differs from district to district.

In some places, the culture views it as fair to preserve the jobs of long-serving staff, but in other communities preserving the income of low-paid staff seems more important, and in other places it just seems fair that local residents who work in the schools get more protection than others.

In the last few years, I'm seeing a new definition of fairness—it's only fair, the thinking goes, that the "most effective" teachers be spared during a reduction in force. Whether it's the proliferation of student growth data, the widespread use of more objective teacher evaluations, the publicity of New York City's rubber room, or the deepening understanding that some teachers are much more effective than others, the trend is growing. To be sure, many people question if we can accurately measure teacher effectiveness, but a number of districts experienced much pushback when they announced cuts that targeted the last hired, without regard to teacher effectiveness.

Protect the Most Effective Teachers

The final option for reducing pushback from budgets that include fewer FTE is by far the most controversial: eliminating the jobs of the least effective. Having worked in the private sector for nearly twenty years before switching to K–12, I had to reduce staffing and everyone expected that top performers were safe and ability would weigh heavily in any cuts. K–12 has, historically, intentionally removed performance from the reduction decision: tenure, seniority, certification, and complex bumping rights determine who stays and who goes.

There are many reasons to include teacher effectiveness when determining staff cuts (e.g., it's better for kids to keep strong teachers), and just as many to exclude it (e.g., the measures of effectiveness are arbitrary and subjective, thus unfair to teachers). A much less common reason might tip the balance. In a number of districts, pushback against reducing staff to fund key priorities was fueled in large part by the widely held belief that the "best teachers" would be let go. Parents and principals alike held this view. Certainly it's no surprise that losing a highly effective teacher would be unpopular, but what was surprising was that these districts had no formal measure of teacher effectiveness, nor had the cuts been finalized, so which teachers exactly might be let go wasn't even known. Turns out, the fear of even potentially losing great teachers generates a lot of angst (as it should).

I recently watched another district easily make some bold staffing moves, cutting in some areas and adding in others, all tightly aligned to its strategic plan. Why such smooth sailing? The district had robust teacher effectiveness data, which was broadly considered a reasonable measure of teacher quality. Their collective bargaining agreement allowed discretion in reductions, and the public assurance that highly effective teachers would not be let go helped assuage principal and parent, and thus school board, pushback.

One cautionary note: in some districts teacher effectiveness data can be as controversial as the cuts themselves, and certainly many union agreements prohibit such an approach. As more states use and refine growth data, this option might become more commonplace.

Reduce Staff Costs Without Reducing Staff

Fighting to preserve jobs will always be a top cause of pushback against smarter budgets, especially as revenues struggle to keep up with expenses. An emerging middle ground is gaining some acceptance. Rather than reduce the number of staff in a given role or department, some districts are finding politically acceptable, but still difficult and unpleasant, ways to reduce costs but not cut positions. To be sure, these options are hard on staff, but not as harsh as outright job loss. These strategies differ from a cut in staffing because the position stays in the budget, but the pay and/or benefits are reduced.

Some districts have walked the tightrope between reducing pay and benefits while minimizing the pushback associated with income loss by incorporating specific actions, not just words, that say *we do value what you do*. These include:

- *Offering more pay and fewer benefits.* One district decided to no longer provide health benefits to paraprofessionals, but paired the benefit cut with a 20 percent raise in hourly pay. The net still saved millions of dollars, but the pay raise signaled a statement of importance to the role. This muted some of the hurt feelings.
- *Valuing the long-serving.* Another district was also contemplating reducing benefits for paraprofessionals. Pushback was fierce, because it seemed like the district was turning its back on many staff who had worked for decades in the district for relatively low wages. Sympathy, especially from principals and school board members, seemed likely to derail the effort. A review of the employment records revealed that only 10 percent of the impacted staff had worked in the district for a very long time; most had five years or less of service. The district did in fact value loyalty and agreed to continue to provide health benefits to all existing staff that had twenty years of service or more. This achieved 90 percent of the savings and reduced the pushback by an equal amount.

Subcontracting can be an option for cutting costs but not head count as well, but it often brings howls of concern about widespread job loss, since in its plainest form it can mean letting go 100 percent of a department or role. Subcontracting custodial-, transportation-, or special education–related services can be a smart financial move, but one that often generates fierce pushback. Worse than dedicated staff losing their jobs, other people actually are getting these jobs! It can seem very unfair. More than a few districts have reduced the pain, and thus the pushback, by protecting the jobs of current staff despite the move to subcontracting.

Some districts have required the subcontractor to hire the existing staff. Wages, benefits, schedules, and work rules typically change, but no one loses their job. A more modest but somewhat helpful middle ground is ensuring that all existing staff get interviewed by the subcontractor. This incorporates aspects of ensuring that the "best" people don't lose their jobs. Other strategies for reducing, but not eliminating, the pain from subcontracting include:

- *Seek gains from managing just benefit costs.* In some situations subcontractors pay their staff the same or better than the school district, but the private sector employer has private sector (less generous) benefits. In this case, a district could issue a request for proposal (RFP) to potential providers that requires them to hire all (or most) of the existing staff and still expect to reduce total costs.
- *Seek gains from managing just restrictive work rules.* Sometimes years of collective bargaining layer many limitations on district staff that aren't common with private sector providers. For example, one district limited speech and language therapists to very small caseloads and provided them extra prep periods. This union-negotiated combination was more generous (costly) than most other districts and all private providers. Subcontracting would eliminate these limitations, and again the district could require current staff to be employed by the new provider.
- *Subcontract only the needed expertise.* Occasionally, the real value and savings from subcontracting comes from

specialized expertise, such as in IT, or from strong management practices as in maintenance or food service. In
these cases, districts can subcontract the management of
a department but keep all the front-line staff.

- *Subcontract to a kinder, smaller employer.* Subcontracting
can hit a nerve with many, because it privatizes a func-
tion traditionally done by a public entity. Making money
from serving schoolchildren may be fine for textbook
companies, but big corporations profiting from subcontracting staff positions is less palatable in some communities. I have seen Fortune 500 food service companies
vilified as feeding on children, rather than feeding them.
To overcome this pushback, some districts have turned
to nonprofits or other municipal agencies as subcontractors. A nonprofit regional special education collaborative,
a nearby school district, or the town HR or IT department can, in some cases, be a more acceptable provider of
subcontracted services.

In addition to the strategies just listed, box 4.1 offers some
insights from the private sector into how school districts might
navigate reducing staffing costs without cutting jobs.

MORE THAN JUST DOLLARS AND CENTS MATTERS

Job and income preservation are obvious and powerful drivers
of pushback and reluctance to shift resources, but the nonfinancial impact on staff of such changes can be equally powerful in preventing student-centered budget decisions from
carrying the day. Often, bruising the self-esteem of staff or undermining their social stability creates equally strong pushback as actual job cuts. Again, any caring organization should

BOX 4.1

CRAZY IDEAS FROM THE PRIVATE SECTOR: REDUCING PAY BUT NOT HEAD COUNT

The private sector has a much longer history of managing reductions in pay, typically forced on it by global competition. The cost of many manufactured goods, adjusted for inflation, has dropped over the years. As consumers we benefited, but the US workers who make these products didn't. Their pay was cut to respond to market forces from Japan, Korea, China, and elsewhere. Given that many of the impacted industries were unionized like most school districts, these firms took steps to lower costs and minimize the impact on their employees. As budgets get ever tighter, school districts might consider borrowing a few pages from their playbook.

- *Shield the lowest-paid staff.* As benefit costs rise, more districts are forced to consider rising copays, deductibles, and premium sharing. Any change to health coverage is contentious, but often clerks, first-year teachers, and other lower-paid staff become the rallying cry for opposition since they will be hardest hit by the change because the increased costs represent a bigger share of their smaller paycheck. Some private sector employers facing a similar situation pair a raise for their lowest-paid staff to help offset the impact of higher employee contributions.
- *New wage structure for new employees only.* Nobel Prize–winning economist John Maynard Keynes noted that wages are downward sticky. This means that economic pressures should push wages up or down, but in reality, wages go up when pressured but are much less likely to go down. In short, people hate seeing their pay cut. Some private sector firms manage this by creating new salary charts for new employees. This is more than just paying new workers less than veterans (the steps in a teacher's contract), a common practice in K–12, but rather creating entirely different pay plans for everyone hired after a given date. This shields all existing employees from the dreaded pay cut, but creates a more financially sustainable system over time.

For example, a teacher hired before September 2015 might start at $45,000 and rise through ten steps and across five lanes to ultimately reach

$80,000 over time. Any teacher hired after September 2015 might also start at $45,000 but might pass through fifteen steps, have fewer lanes, and max out at $70,000. The latter teacher's pay would rise more slowly and not reach the same peak. It's very common in unionized manufacturing plants, for example, to see new employees doing the same job as long-serving ones, but being paid less. This certainly raises issues of fairness, but it allows for pay scales to be reset to the new fiscal realities without the pushback of a pay cut for existing staff. Also, everyone hired under the new plan knows and accepts it in advance—no surprises after the fact.

It's easy to dismiss the idea of dual pay scales as not applicable to K–12 given the historic practice that everyone gets paid the same—effective or not, core subject or not. Interestingly, a version of this is already being widely used in education. For example, every teacher in Massachusetts hired after July 1, 2001, got a pay cut compared to those hired beforehand. It was a bit subtle, in that newly hired teachers contribute more to their pensions than those already working and will receive less generous pensions when they retire. The state needed to shore up its pension fund and realized that a big increase in contribution and cut to benefits would likely create much angst, so it opted to apply the higher rate only to new employees, who didn't actually see it as a reduction in take-home pay, since it's all they knew. This equates to a two-tiered system of pay.

Other districts have created two-tiered pay systems, but vary the form of compensation—such as performance pay rather than steps and lanes. Existing staff can opt in, but newly hired staff must be on the new pay plan.

value the feelings of its members, and can take steps to move funds in a respectful manner.

The most compelling case in point, and by no means an outlier, was a district that made the strategic decision to have students with special needs be taught by certified math teachers with deep content expertise, not by generalists like special education teachers, who lacked training and expertise in math. To minimize the impact on staff (or so the district leaders thought) they decided to phase in the change only through attrition. As special educators retired or moved away, the district would hire more math teachers. No one lost their job, but unfortunately many lost face. The pushback was as fierce and tenacious as if hundreds were losing their jobs (remember, *no one* lost their job). The staff wrote letters to the school board, called reporters, and attended school board meetings en masse. They were insulted and weren't going to take this lying down. Ironically, this resistance was led by a cadre of very senior teachers. Had the district simply laid off a few untenured teachers instead, it might have generated less anger, since the veterans would be spared the impact of the layoffs.

Nonfinancial pain can generate much pushback for two reasons. First, while reduction in force impacts only a few people in a department—say, one in twenty staff members might be let go—the entire group (i.e., all twenty staff members) can feel insulted that their department or program is being cut. The other reason is that the district might actually be stating, through its actions, "Your department or role isn't as important as others," which is often heard as "*You* aren't as important as others."

This second reason really seems to strike a nerve in many people. Having worked about half my life in the private sector and the other half in K–12, I've noticed that one of the greatest differences revolves around the notion of focus. Through much of my business life, books, conferences, graduate programs, and consultants extolled the value of setting a few priorities and concentrating on doing them well. *You can't do everything* was the mantra. Well-run organizations constantly refined and narrowed their focus.

As a school district leader, I felt constantly under pressure to do it all—add more foreign languages, more time for learning, and more time for teacher collaboration; raise math scores and improve social awareness; provide coteaching, pullout, and afterschool support; address obesity; and provide free preK. I wanted to do all of these and more, because I knew children needed all of this, yet at the same time I was convinced we lacked the funds to do everything and the capacity to do everything *well*.

Shrinking budgets are forcing school district leaders to pick and choose, to focus more than ever. Gone are the days when a new reading program could be added and the old one also kept in place. Implementing a readers' workshop means ending reading recovery. As dollars shrink further, districts must decide if having a longer school day or smaller classes matters more, since they can't afford both. Budget deliberations are now more often about setting priorities, and resource allocation decisions are public statements about what is valued most in a district.

For staff working in departments or programs lower on the priority list (less important, but not unimportant), it can feel insulting or like a personal affront, and certainly seem worth fighting over. Some districts have developed a number of ways to minimize the impact on staff self-esteem and perceived worth when having to prioritize other spending.

The key lies in crafting a communication plan to ensure the deserved dignity. One district, which had relied heavily on paraprofessionals to teach reading to struggling students, made the strategic decision to shift instruction to highly skilled and certified reading teachers. At the cabinet meeting the discussion went like this:

Superintendent: We owe it to our struggling students to provide the most skilled teachers we can hire. Paras aren't even teachers at all.

C&I director: Teaching reading is an art, as well as a skill. Just because someone can read doesn't make them an effective reading teacher. Our emphasis on noncertified paras and tutors hasn't closed our achievement gap and we shouldn't expect they can.

Title I director: My paras work hard and many live in town. We can't just hang them out to dry.

Despite the Title I director's concerns, the decision to reduce the number of paraprofessionals was made. Unfortunately, when presenting a budget with more reading teachers and fewer paraprofessionals, the superintendent justified the decision publicly with the same language used in the cabinet meetings: "We owe it to our struggling students to provide the most skilled teachers we can hire. Paras aren't teachers."

To minimize the impact on staff, many of the paras displaced by the decision would be offered positions elsewhere in the district in special education or covering school duties. This effort to soften the blow addressed financial loss, but not loss of face. The paras pushed back hard; even parents of struggling readers who would benefit most from the changes rushed to support the paras and blocked the shift. Nice people had been insulted, and their friends weren't going to stand by and idly watch.

Another superintendent, wanting to make the same change, framed the decision in a more respectful way. "The Common Core is coming and its emphasis on close reading ups the ante greatly," he said. "The district must respond, if all of our children are going to be prepared and successful at the higher standards." While each superintendent was motivated by similar theories of action, the second, in essence, validated the past (implying that what they had was fine, until this change was forced upon them). This was not an attack on paras, but a response to a new reality. Importantly, the paraprofessionals weren't specifically mentioned in the framing. This was about the Common Core, not paras. To further this point, the budget presentation bundled dollars for reading professional development in this new line item, not in the PD section, to highlight that everyone, including classroom teachers, would need to do things differently given the coming of the Common Core.

Another face-saving strategy is to clearly place the blame (the need for the change) outside the district, often on the state department of education. Continuing with the previous example, the message could also include the following: "The Common Core has in other states doubled the number of students identified as struggling. If that happens to us, the state might be more likely to designate many of our schools as 'in need of improvement.' We must ensure nearly all of our students can read at grade level or suffer state intervention."

Avoid Across-the-Board Reductions

Shifting limited resources toward best practices and strategic priorities does message that some uses of funds are better than others. Well-crafted communications can help minimize the personal hurt that comes with being placed on the less critical side of the ledger. Some districts, however, take protecting staff self-esteem and self-worth too far, and they may not realize that this is leading them to the worst of all budget decisions: the across-the-board budget cut. An across-the-board reduction signals a lack of focus, priorities, or clear theory of action: it says that everything is equally important and equally effective. While this is seldom true, across-the-board cuts are common nonetheless. Their popularity stems from their highly effective face-saving qualities. Nothing is singled out as less important, so pushback is muted—but so is student learning.

The allure of across-the-board cuts is strong. One superintendent realized that with an enrollment bubble passing through the district, extra staff hired a number of years ago to serve the swelling elementary schools was no longer needed, and more staff was needed now at the secondary level, as these large cohorts got older. While the need for more middle and high school teachers and fewer elementary ones was clear, the district balked at making the shift. A few years passed, and the problem became more extreme, with classes of seventeen or eighteen in the overstaffed elementary school and twenty-six to thirty in the understaffed middle school, despite class size targets of twenty-four. To complicate matters, tax revenues weren't keeping up with expenses, so budget cuts were needed. The superintendent suggested some modest trimming at the elementary schools, but no additions at the secondary level, because it "didn't seem fair to add to some schools while cutting others." Ultimately, small across-the-board cuts were passed to balance the budget, because the school board didn't want to "target" the pain just at some schools but not others. Interestingly, they hadn't had a problem, years earlier, just adding staff in the younger grades as enrollment grew.

Make the Case for Change

Spending money differently often means doing things differently. While change is not as traumatic as losing a job, income, or face, K–12 staff have been on a merry-go-round of change for decades and more change isn't without its own pain. Beyond the desire for stability, change in K–12 has an added burden: the fear that the change won't really help students or that it isn't actually needed. Why subject staff to discomfort, why move their cheese, why cause good people to move from the schools they like or end programs they adore if things are going well, or at least as well as can reasonably be expected?

Too often, leaders advocating for spending money and time differently *assume* others share their sense for the need for change. Making such an assumption has inadvertently stymied many good ideas. No Child Left Behind, state accountability systems, and school ratings have provided an unprecedented level of data on how well students, schools, or district are doing, but they haven't helped bring about much *agreement* on how well students, schools, or districts are doing. It is hard for people to embrace hard decisions if they feel that the status quo is working okay as is.

One superintendent, determined to close the achievement gap in reading for students of poverty, students with special needs, and students learning English, proposed some big shifts in funding to address a large and growing gap. As a champion for social justice, he assumed everyone shared his concern and that all would understand the need to move funds and, unfortunately, impact some existing staff positions. To the superintendent's surprise, few supported the changes. On deeper review, he learned that since most kids in the district were doing well, there was a general sense of accomplishment, so supporting a hard decision wasn't in the cards.

Contentment with the status quo can be found in the lowest performing schools and districts as well. One district, for example, operating under tight state supervision and sanctioned as chronically underperforming, exhibited nearly identical comfort with current practices and results. To be fair, staff weren't pleased with proficiency rates in the low teens or even single digits, and didn't like being ranked in the bottom 2 percent of all districts in the state, but they were "okay" with it, just the same. In candid conversations with staff, principals, and central office leaders, I learned that many felt the district was doing as well as could be expected. They explained that the district had very little money (not true) and that the student population had shifted dramatically toward students living in poverty and non-native English speakers (true). The district re-sults reflected this reality and no new spending plan, no shifts in strategy, and no resources would change this. No, they did not see any reason to support a highly disruptive budget.

Give Staff Time to Question and Reflect

Another strategy for helping to overcome staff's desire for sta-bility is to give them time to get used to the change before im-plementing it. I have been surprised by how many good budget shifts that previously died a painful death sail through a year or two later with relative ease. It seems that time to process a proposed change can have three benefits:

1. Time to ask questions
2. Time to research answers
3. Time to calm down

On the flip side, a slow deliberate process also gives time to harden one's stance and fan the flames, but this typically happens whether you move quickly or slowly. The typical bud-get building calendar doesn't usually provide staff time to get comfortable with an uncomfortable change.

Most districts start budget planning in the late fall, present initial ideas in the winter, and finalize the tough decisions a few months later. Often staff have about four to eight weeks to learn the details of the final recommendations, process them, and mobilize if needed. As it turns out, this is plenty of time to dislike an idea, but maybe not enough time to really under-stand it.

Big changes announced at a school board meeting or public forum can't answer every small detailed question, such as "What about students who . . . ?" "What about the grant that commits us to . . . ?" "What about staff that are certified in . . . ?" District leaders respond to these queries the best they can, but often rumor and misinformation provide many of the answers first. Sometimes, thoughtful questions can't be answered without more research or planning, and less-than-compelling answers like "We will look into it" or "We will take that into consideration as we work out the details later" seldom calm fears even if the ultimate answers are reassuring.

Perhaps more problematic than not having enough time to ask and answer questions is when the timing itself is bad. Just as you shouldn't grocery-shop when hungry, talking about big or strategic budget changes during budget season is not best. Staff are tense, and stakes and emotions run high. The staff most impacted by any changes may not be in a good frame of mind to hear and process your answers to their questions.

One district avoided the rush by announcing the change nearly a year in advance, and then had lots of time to address staff concerns. Its goal was to revamp dropout prevention efforts, which included changing who provided many of these services and shifting to a "tough love" approach to students failing classes—pushing for high rigor rather than easy-to-pass alternatives. The initial reaction from guidance counselors and high school staff was very negative. But as the year went on, virtually every week there was a reminder of how current efforts were failing, and how the new services might be better. Equally importantly, monthly dialogue raised questions and provided detailed answers that calmed many fears. The changes were implemented a year later with little pushback, and graduation rates increased by thirteen points over five years.

Start with Volunteers

It's helpful to acknowledge that some people are already more comfortable with change than others. An interesting hallmark of resistance to budgetary changes is the asymmetry of the struggle. A few people who may be very negatively impacted have enormous energy and motivation to mount an attack on the change. The benefits, on the other hand, are often widely diffused, and thus don't create an equally energized counterforce. Staff who want stability will work hard, very hard, to preserve it.

Margaret Mead said, "Never believe that a few caring people can't change the world. For, indeed, that's all who ever have." Had she visited my middle school, she might have quipped, "Never believe that a few unhappy people can't stop the world from changing, for indeed that happens every year around budget time."

I remember vividly (with cold sweats) the reaction to my decision to decrease coteaching by special educators and increase extra math classes taught by certified math teachers. The logic was strong. Coteaching had led to huge achievement gaps in the district, and the national research wasn't encouraging either. In our schools that adopted double classes taught by general education teachers, learning and scores skyrocketed.

Two veteran special education teachers at the middle school loved coteaching and felt insulted by the implication that others (math teachers) could teach math more effectively. They called every school committee member repeatedly, they presented at every school board meeting, they wrote letters to the editor of the local paper, they phoned dozens of parents saying their students were being kicked out of class midyear (not even remotely true), and they informed the department of education that the district was about to illegally void hundreds of IEPs. Not surprisingly, the firestorm scuttled the change and the school drifted into state sanctions for chronically low achievement in math by students with special needs.

The irony is, many—maybe even most—of the special educators in the school welcomed the change. They knew achievement was low due to prior sanctions by the state, felt underprepared to teach math, and were often treated with disrespect by their coteaching partners. "I'm treated like a paraprofessional, not a teacher," one shared with me. Their willingness to go along with the change didn't translate into them calling, writing, and lobbying for change, though. They sat this fight out.

A few years later, seeing an eerily similar situation in a middle school of a client, I cautioned the superintendent from moving too quickly, since a diehard group of teachers also loved coteaching despite extremely low achievement. Wiser than I, he suggested, "Let's make the change voluntary." "For students?" I asked, a bit puzzled. "No, for teachers," he replied.

He had surveyed the situation and realized that just like in my district, some teachers would fight to the death to maintain the status quo, and others did see the benefits. He avoided the pushback by asking the teachers individually if they wanted to participate in the change, and assured them that none of them would lose their jobs regardless of their decisions. More than half said yes, and through attrition enough dollars were saved to pay for the math teachers. First-year successes led to increased pressure on the remaining coteachers to expand the new approach.

Some may have trouble with a strategy of easing change by starting with the willing: "If it's right for students, then damn it, we should do it for all students." While this may be the moral high ground, it got me no change in my middle school. My colleague's phased approach helped more students. The "start with volunteers" approach allows the most vocal opponents to stay calm and eases the way forward. I have seen the approach work well with rolling out a new curriculum, ending ineffective programs, redesigning the role of instructional coaching, awarding performance pay, outlining new approaches to professional development, managing the use of paraprofessionals, and enacting many other good-for-kids resource reallocation plans.

Since sometimes it's principals, not teachers, who lead the resistance, starting with willing schools is a similarly effective approach. The thing to watch for here, however, is that parents can react poorly to inequity between schools. Positioning the first year as a pilot can help.

5

WIN OVER SUPPORTERS THROUGH JOINT FACT FINDING

A Formal Process of Building Shared Understanding Can End Many Budget Fights Before They Start

It's easy to understand why many people resist painful but student-centric changes to spending. Differing theories of action and differing definitions of success breed opposition because different people actually want different things. Others resist because friends and colleagues will be hurt, but another common reason good people fight thoughtful change to spending is because many of the opponents have a different fact base, suggesting a particular change isn't needed, isn't legal, or has never worked. Given their understanding of the facts, they are simply resisting a very bad idea.

The view from the leadership perch can make the need for change seem obvious, such as "If only 50 percent of our students graduate, the achievement gap between poor and not poor is stubbornly large," or "Revenue has dropped by 6 percent." In high and low performing districts alike, areas for improvement or financial realities can seemingly scream for change. When I have taken the time, built a trusting space, and listened to front-line staff, I have been surprised by why they opposed any number of my changes. Yes, some concerns were rooted in job preservation, self-esteem, or differing theories of action, but very often they simply didn't see the same problems as the leadership team. A few startling examples include:

- I knew that we faced a $3.2 million deficit, so something must be cut, but they saw a state-of-the-art exercise room just installed (from a grant) and rising property values, suggesting very flush times.
- I knew that our teachers were paid more than like communities, except in the first few years in the district, and they knew teachers who left the district for $10,000 pay increases.
- I knew that our students of color and with disabilities achieved at low levels, and they knew this was true in most districts.

In all these cases, and many more, our differing set of facts made agreement impossible, support unrealistic, and even dialogue difficult. Once I realized how different our facts were, I set out to fix these misunderstandings. I prepared charts, tables, graphs, and memos to share the truth and explain the situation. Unfortunately, this only made matters worse. They questioned every number, took exception to most conclusions, and offered up vague but contrary data, often in the form of an anecdote about a person or student they knew. The anxiety and friction actually increased as a result of these communication efforts.

A much more effective approach to building a common understanding walked into my office one day. A town resident and former professor of negotiations at MIT made an appointment to see me. He commented that everyone seems to have good intentions, but bad feelings. I recounted to him all the explaining I was doing, and he noted that I was sharing facts with others, but they were "my facts" and thus wouldn't be persuasive. "Facts are facts," I pointed out. "That's the very nature of facts!" I said, self-satisfied.

After reminding me of how ineffective my approach had been at winning over converts, he suggested an alternative: formal *joint fact finding*. Details to follow shortly, but let me lead with the ending . . . it worked miracles time and time again.

REDUCE PUSHBACK THROUGH
JOINT FACT FINDING

The concept of joint fact finding is deceptively simple. Through a structured process, allow district leaders and representatives of those impacted by the potential change under consideration and their colleagues to gather the facts together, and to challenge the facts all along the way.

Our first try with this strategy focused on a long-standing, emotionally charged, big-ticket line item: teacher compensation. Collective bargaining was to begin soon, the budget was shrinking, and our starting pay made it hard to attract new teachers, but our veteran staff were paid well. We couldn't afford to raise everyone's pay by a lot, so I wanted a bigger increase at the bottom of the pay scale, but a small bump (or none) at the top. This plan was declared dead on arrival since the teachers believed that veterans were dramatically underpaid and the town had money to raise everyone to parity with like communities. This expectation was just fair and decent, not greedy, in the teachers' worldview. Interestingly, if their facts were right, their ideas were reasonable.

With the help of an independent facilitator, a joint fact finding committee was formed. It included district leaders, teachers with a wide range of seniority (from just a few years' experience to more than thirty), and a couple of school board members. The committee's charge was to collect the facts, not solve the problem, specifically to answer the one question: How do our teacher salaries compare to like communities?

The first meeting was awful. We, the district administrators, pulled out our analysis and the teachers brought their own. Almost immediately, both sides started justifying their position and debunking the other. The committee had jumped straight to an answer, albeit differing answers. But for a skillful facilitator, I doubt a second meeting would have taken place. At his urging, we all took a deep breath and a step back. "What defines a like community?" the facilitator asked. We began listing nearby towns. "Stop," demanded the facilitator. "Pay attention to the question—what defines a like community? Not 'which communities are like ours?'"

Working independently, each side created lists of criteria. It seemed pretty simple. When we shared the lists, however, it turned out to be anything but straightforward. The district leaders' criteria included per-pupil spending, average family income, and percent free and reduced lunch in the same state but excluding the rural towns hours away. The teachers' list had little overlap! They included student test scores and graduation rates in nonurban areas and within a fifteen-mile radius. Sharing the lists revealed our first common understanding: we didn't agree on what constituted a like community. Essentially, the district leaders gave weight to economic factors, and the teachers prioritized other districts they might consider working in. These differences mattered a lot, since our middle-class, lower-than-average-spending district was surrounded by either urban districts with lots of state aid or very affluent, high spending districts.

If we were ever to agree on which communities were like ours, we would need to take a few steps back. Over the next three months, the joint fact finding team engaged in a deep exploration of municipal finance. The town manager, finance committee members from neighboring towns, and independent experts detailed the town's past, present, and future finances and those of other communities. Fully fifteen hours of learning and questioning took place. Many pushed back at how much time was being "wasted" on unrelated research, but the town's ability to pay was critical to deciding which communities were like ours. Oddly, no one ever felt fifteen hours of head-to-head negotiations was wasteful, even if it wasn't fruitful. In the end we agreed—not just compromised, but actually *agreed*—that household income mattered, as did proximity of about an hour's drive.

With common criteria established, a subcommittee collected data on every town within an hour's drive to find the similar communities. When the list was presented jointly by the subcommittee, all hell broke loose again! Everyone not on the subcommittee was certain that some other town should be added or dropped. Rather than get defensive, the facilitator encouraged this debate. Any person could challenge the list, suggesting deleting or adding a town. Over the next month, each challenge was reviewed with the entire committee and the data and analysis reviewed, right down to the source documents. Some unbelievers were tasked with calling town managers directly to confirm that the state-provided data was accurate. This step seemed tedious and insulting. But it was critical. In time, everyone agreed on the list.

Months later, when the list was shared publicly, all the same objections resurfaced by others not on the joint fact finding committee: "ABC township doesn't belong" and "Why was XYZ-ville excluded?" Fortunately, we already had answers to these questions, and the teachers on the committee quickly verified the answers to be true (even if surprising). As it turned out, the town oft-quoted by teachers as paying $10,000 more was also twice as well-off, and funded its schools 50 percent more per pupil. It wasn't a like community, even if it was nearby and had a similar-looking downtown.

With an agreed-upon list in hand, the committee compared salaries between like communities. It took five months to get to this point, a long slog, but it took only a few hours for all to see that our new teachers were underpaid by about $3,000 and veterans earned about $3,500 more than like communities. The union proposed a sophisticated face-saving idea: drop the first step, give a fixed dollar increase rather than a percent increase (percent increases give more dollars to higher paid staff—e.g., 3 percent to a new teacher earning $40,000 is $1,200, but 3 percent to a veteran earning $70,000 is $2,100), and reduce longevity payments while grandfathering in current staff.

The final plan wasn't perfect, but it did address about half the gap, didn't cost any more than a typical raise, and was achieved with little anger. It was slow, however.

In the years that followed, I have seen joint fact finding pave the way for bold, seemingly unpopular budget reallocations for librarians, paraprofessionals, math intervention, reading programs, social workers, and many more. In all cases, the process took time and required much patience to embrace the questions, as well as an open mind. Box 5.1 outlines some tips for

BOX 5.1

TIPS FOR SUCCESSFUL
JOINT FACT FINDING

Joint fact finding can build strong support for typically unpopular budget shifts, but shortcuts or missteps can undermine the process. It's very hard to restore trust once it's lost.

- *Weeks or months prior to presenting a recommendation, present and share widely the analysis that guided your decision making.* When you put the agreed-upon facts out in public first, questions about the facts will arise and can be answered before the actual plan is presented (and challenged). For stakeholders who could go either way—support or oppose—this can swing many of them. It's hard to convert a no to a yes, and laying the groundwork in advance prevents many from jumping to "no" because their facts differ.
- *Share all the background data from the beginning.* In the era of Power-Point, we are prone to share only the conclusions of our research in a single chart or a few bullets. Back in the day, we might have written a full report and then stuffed twenty pages of background data in an appendix. Doubters could comb through the raw data and draw their own conclusions, which often were the same as those presented. PowerPoint isn't going away, but we can still share the background data, perhaps posting it to the district website (when appropriate).
- *Be careful not to collect bad data.* Good decisions are based on good data, but not all the information living in district computers is accurate, and questioning its validity is an easy way to discredit an uncomfortable truth.

    This caution has been most helpful when it comes to managing special education, since district databases are often inaccurate or incomplete and the variation from teacher to teacher or building to building is great. By having every special education teacher, aide, therapist, and psychologist share from their own hand a typical week's schedule, for example, districts have been able to dramatically streamline and improve special education services, with limited pushback.

continues

Such studies have highlighted ineffective service delivery models, excessive time in meetings, widely different expectations for how much paperwork is needed, and so on. Few staff would have believed it if the central office said, "Our research indicates many staff are in meetings and doing paperwork more than working with children," but when the data comes from the teachers themselves it becomes much more believable.

making the joint fact finding process as smooth and successful as possible.

BUILD SUPPORT THROUGH JOINT FACT FINDING

Joint fact finding can be a powerful, albeit slow, tool for reducing pushback, as in the teacher compensation example. It can also be helpful in building support, which isn't exactly the same as reducing pushback. As already mentioned, having those most impacted by the potential changes participate in the joint fact finding can help them more readily accept the results and their implications. This is a good step, but it's not often sufficient. Even if the facts prove beyond a shadow of a doubt that librarians provide very little benefit to students and have many free hours a day, the librarians aren't likely to energetically support halving their number. They may better understand the decision, but they will still likely fight it with gusto. Their reaction doesn't undermine the benefit of joint fact finding, however; it just shifts it.

When my district did study the role and staffing levels of our elementary librarians we, of course, had many of the librarians on the joint fact finding committee, but we also had many other staff, such as principals, reading teachers, and influential and open-minded classroom teachers. Toward the end, when the librarians (understandably) pushed back, these other committee members believed the facts justified the decision to reduce staffing and downgrade the position. They knew from their work on the committee that:

- half the librarians had only a part-time workload but got full-time pay;
- librarians taught only ten hours of direct instruction a year, and mostly managed checking books in and out; and
- librarians had no role in the district's flagship reading program.

These facts didn't sit well with other teachers. They worked full-time, devoted countless hours to reading instruction each week, and more. They lost sympathy and enthusiasm for maintaining the status quo. When others rushed to support the librarians, these committee members shared the facts quietly and persuasively. Ultimately, support for the change was strong and pushback limited to a handful of librarians. This was a marked contrast to the year earlier, when a similar proposal created a firestorm of backlash from a broad base of teachers and parents, and the plan was shelved.

TRACK KPIS AS A REAL-TIME FORM OF JOINT FACT FINDING

Joint fact finding is often a one-off project. A special need leads to a special committee. It's slow and consumes many hours from busy people. *Key performance indicators*, or KPIs in the lingo, can be a form of constantly updated joint fact finding. These are specific measures of a system's performance, often measured against history and benchmarked against like organizations or a goal.

It might seem more common to discuss KPIs in a book on strategic planning than in one on winning support for tough budget decisions, but good, mutually agreed-upon KPIs can win over supporters for tough budget decisions. Good KPIs take time to develop, and it's best if they are not developed during the budget season or, initially, not linked to spending. At their core, they should represent relevant ways to measure success.

In the case of the district mentioned in chapter 4 that significantly raised graduation rates over five years, joint fact finding helped start the process, but thoughtful KPIs also played an important role. Rather than just tracking and reporting graduation rates, which had been very public but not sufficient to win support for shifting resources despite the unimpressive results, the district tracked more persuasive data. It turned out that when staff saw the low graduation rates, they had a few facts of their own, including:

- most students who dropped out transferred into the district late in their education;
- many students who dropped out had significant learning disabilities; and
- the alternative programs offered by the district were helping a lot to keep students in school.

Knowing that these were widely believed "facts" that undermined support for change, and if true, perhaps not as much change was need, the district began to track some new KPIs:

- Graduation rate by number of years a student was in the district
- Dropout rates based on level of disability (none, mild, or severe)
- Graduation rate of students in selected alternative programs

As with joint fact finding, key stakeholders such as the high school leadership and guidance department were active in helping create the very fine detail of how this data would be gathered and how the stats would be calculated. With this high level of involvement up front, it was easier for them to believe the numbers.

The KPIs revealed a fact base very different from common wisdom and lore. Most students who dropped out had been in the district for at least six years, many even longer; students without disabilities dropped out at similar rates to those with disabilities; and most students in alternative programs didn't graduate. These facts galvanized a desire to change and helped fine-tune decisions in years to come. Even the typically highly charged decision to subcontract was relatively stress-free. Consistent KPI data indicating that the alternative programs offered by the district weren't up to the task eased the way for turning over management of some alternative programs to a third party.

Effective KPIs measure what's important, and they measure it in a way that is compelling to key stakeholders. Defaulting to state-defined metrics seldom motivates staff. Carefully crafting what's measured, the source of data, and the points of comparison is key.

Another district, content that it outperformed most districts in the state, also created some compelling KPIs that created support for spending differently. It measured elementary math performance compared to both English language arts (ELA) performance at the elementary level and math performance at the secondary level. When the KPIs indicated that its elementary students outperformed most like districts in elementary English and its secondary students also outperformed similar students in math, the district came to recognize that the elementary math program and/or instruction wasn't as good as it could be since the elementary math KPI placed it eighteenth of twenty in the comparison group. Without the relative measures and other KPIs, staff had assumed that given the students they had they were doing the best they could, which wasn't bad compared to most districts in the state. When they realized that their very same students did much better in English and excelled in math in the secondary grades, their facts and motivation changed.

The district made some tough budget decisions to invest in extensive training: adopting new hiring practices, including targeting teachers at higher steps and lanes if the candidate had strong math credentials; removing paraprofessional math tutors; and adding math interventionists. Not only did the changes pass without much pushback (except from the tutors), but within a few years math scores skyrocketed, raising district achievement from eighteenth to eighth in the elementary students' peer group and doubling the number of students scoring advanced over four years.

Good implementation and good teaching made the difference, but shifting dollars fueled the effort. Kick-starting it all, however, was a thoughtful set of key performance indicators that built support for the change in spending and staffing by creating a shared understanding of current needs and performance.

BUILD A COMMON FACT BASE THROUGH
FORMAL PROGRAM EVALUATIONS

Effective KPIs require ongoing measurement against both history and a standard. Another, perhaps easier-to-start approach to the same end is to announce and implement a formal, structured process for program evaluation. A methodical, dispassionate, and patient process of evaluating what's working, for which students, cost-effectively can help stakeholders understand why some changes in spending are being recommended. We'll cover one such model next.

A key aspect of formal program review is the calendar of the review process. If you want to have a change in place at the start of the school year in September 2015, it must be part of the budget plan that's built in January 2015, but the first steps for this change must begin in January 2014, some *twenty months* before the change might take effect. This isn't because some changes take a great deal of planning; this is just enough time to build a common understanding of why the change is needed.

Some people need time to research the facts and time to get comfortable with an idea—to ask questions, do more research, and receive thoughtful answers. Because no dispassionate discussions take place during the budget development cycle, the program evaluation cycle should begin more than a year in advance.

Normalizing change and getting staff, leaders, and the community comfortable with change (and thus deescalating pushback) should start with a review of achievement and cost data. Which student needs are unmet? What trends are going in the wrong direction? What costs are growing? What strategic priorities aren't making headway? For certain, many districts formally or informally ask these questions, often around

November or December as they start to build next year's budget. The twist in this alternative approach of formal program evaluation is that these questions and answers are intended to influence not next year's budget, but the budget a year after that—the one that starts in twenty months.

This can seem awfully early to start reviewing and planning. Why such a long process? Because the shorter process too often leads to pushback and minimal change. The longer road can get you to your desired destination quicker, because the shorter path too often is a dead end.

Some districts I have worked with have had much success with the "plan and review early" approach. A typical scheduling might be: In January 2014 the leadership team identifies two to four programs, strategies, or topics for review. One is not enough, because it will feel to the potentially impacted stakeholders that they are being picked on, singled out for attack. Selecting multiple areas for review avoids this and begins to set the pattern that review doesn't automatically mean something negative.

During February through April, not much (related to this process) happens. Why? Because this is when budgets are being built, debated, and vetted. There is no worse time to research program effectiveness than during the height and heat of budget season. It is a good time, however, for the school board to vote to approve the to-be-reviewed list. This adds validation to the topics to be studied, signals a year in advance that changes to these programs *might* be coming, and sets the expectation that detailed data and recommendations are now expected by the school board. Also, as the leadership team wrestles with crafting the next budget, there is often more support for having more and better information, even if it is not for the current challenge at hand.

In spring 2014, pretty much the day after the 2014–2015 budget is passed, it's time to start the program review on the two to four topics or programs selected for study to impact the 2015–2016 budget. The program reviews can utilize many of the joint fact finding strategies previously detailed.

By the end of the summer of 2014, the analysis and conclusions should be drawn. The summer is a great time for thoughtfully studying what's working, and what's not. Since budget season is not around the corner, motives (and the findings) are less likely to be questioned.

Early fall 2014 is when the findings (the facts, but not the implications of the facts), but not the recommendations, should be shared ("This is what we learned . . ."). Stakeholders can ask questions, more research can be conducted, and findings will be updated throughout the fall.

In January 2015, some twelve months after the process began, it's time to report what was learned and which changes will be incorporated into the budget for 2015–2016. See figure 5.1 for a complete timeline of the budget planning process.

The long process won't take the sting out of any cutbacks, nor will it quell pushback from the people directly impacted. It will, however, have helped everyone else. The process won't feel arbitrary. The facts won't be doubted by others, and interestingly, many—including the school board—will have come to expect something to change in a few of these programs. It helps greatly, as well, if at least one of the four topics has a finding of "Fine as is," or even "Expand." Review shouldn't be camouflage for cutting.

Finally, and most importantly, is to repeat the process again and again. If a district cycles through this approach for a few years, expectations and culture come to accept that programs will be reviewed often, and changed as dictated by the cost and

FIGURE 5.1
Budget planning timeline

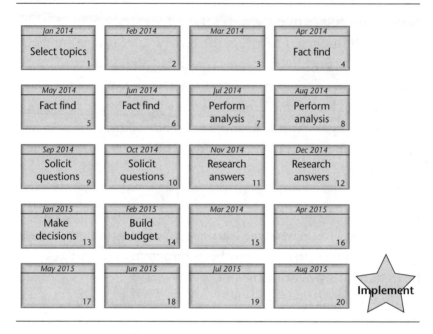

outcomes data. When done well, this cycle of review and modification can feel uplifting and student-centered.

Honest, calm program review has many benefits. It keeps a focus on results. It messages that efforts that are successful receive continued funding and that less effective efforts are cut, reduced, or altered. If this happens year after year, it also feels less personal, less emotional, and more normal.

BUILD REVIEW IN FROM THE START

A powerful way to normalize and depersonalize program review and the related changes to what's funded is to schedule reviews into all new big funding decisions from the get-go. Since so much of the pushback can stem from the question

"Why are you targeting (picking on) my program?" it's helpful to set the expectation up front that for ethical and fiscal reasons, most new programs will be reviewed after six months or every year. If the district is funding a new dropout prevention effort, then make funding contingent on a program review after six months, one year, and two years. While no one funds a new effort thinking it will fail, don't we owe it to students to know for certain that it's helping more of them graduate, and shouldn't the school board know how much it is spending per additional graduate?

Another plus of scheduling future reviews as part of today's funding decisions is that it forces the discussion of how success will be measured before the dollars are spent. This requirement creates a world of good. When measures of success are defined in advance, it's easier to evaluate the decision to spend money in the first place and easier to stop spending money in the future if the data indicates that the intended purpose isn't being accomplished.

The final noteworthy benefit of setting the definition of success at the time of funding is that it can shape the program rollout in a way that's easier to measure, and thus the future review findings will be more widely accepted. When efforts to cut or expand a program are challenged, a common argument is that the measures used to justify the decision are faulty. "Yes, scores went up, but it's due to the teachers, not the program, so there's no need to spend more on it to expand it to other grades or schools," or "Yes, scores went down, but the children served are increasingly needy, so it's not an indication that we need to end the funding."

The most troubling aspect of this kind of "I don't believe your analysis, so I don't support your change" pushback is that the agitated stakeholders are often right! Analyzing program effectiveness and teasing out the isolated impact of the program is hard, unless evaluation is built into the rollout from the start. A few relatively simple steps on day one can make the future evaluation much more accurate and persuasive. This includes mandating a baseline assessment to enable measures of student growth, rolling out the effort in some classrooms or schools to create a control group, or not trying multiple new efforts with the same children. If new programs are designed to be fairly evaluated, based on yardsticks agreed upon in advance, then it's easy for all involved to accept the findings, and shift, expand, or cut funding based on the program review.

This approach of normalizing review, and shifting resources as a result, can feel unworkable to some educators, but it's a well-established practice in other sectors. Nonprofits working to end malaria or HIV rigorously monitor all their efforts, roll them out in ways that allow for easy measurement of effectiveness, and employ many staff dedicated to measuring program effectiveness. They want to know what works, and stop what isn't, because lives are at stake. The stakes are equally high in K–12.

Formalizing a process of review and abandonment was refined and scaled at General Electric when it faced problems very similar to many public school districts, and its evolution could guide district efforts. The company had many products and, as the world changed, added new products and services much faster than it ended old ones. Stakeholders grew concerned that resources were being spread thin, often on efforts that were no longer top priorities or effective.

How often do districts roll out a new behavior program or reading intervention, but fail to end the existing ones? At first, GE had no greater luck than many school districts. It asked leaders to identify candidates for review and abandonment, and only a token few made the list. GE's leaders, it seemed, were better at defending their turf than trimming it.

Their next step was to set consistent, rigorous measures of how to gauge the performance of its many products and services. Armed with accurate and consistent data, leaders and managers had a much clearer picture of what was successful and what wasn't. The list of things to stop or expand grew as a result. They next formalized the process with a separate department devoted to managing the collection, sharing, and reviewing of performance data on a fixed calendar. As they formalized the review process, the culture started to shift. Ending something that wasn't needed or wasn't as successful as a similar effort became a sign of strength, not weakness. Product division leaders actively used the data to ferret out candidates to cull or trim.

Why did they change their turf-protecting ways? For a few reasons. Certainly, having honest data helped, but incentives were also aligned. As they trimmed in one area, they freed up funds for other, more promising or successful efforts. They viewed the process as shifting, not just cutting. Secondly, turf-protecting managers couldn't get promoted. Ending what wasn't working became a key component of performance reviews.

Perhaps most encouraging is that the formal process of review and abandonment allowed the company to grow and prosper at unprecedented levels. Its success can be attributed in large part to its discipline in funding what was wise to fund, stopping old efforts no longer needed, or fixing or ending less successful ideas. The value of abandonment became so obvious to the former turf-protecting leaders that at the company's next evolutionary step the separate department charged with managing and monitoring such reviews was no longer needed. The managers and leaders each took the responsibility on themselves. An extra department wasn't needed anymore because leaders *wanted* to know what was worth continuing and what wasn't. No one had to make them do it.

Perhaps someday, most principals, department heads, and central office leaders will also aggressively seek the data to know for sure what to stop funding and where to invest the freed-up dollars. Box 5.2 provides some resources for helping determine what's working.

BOX 5.2

KNOWING WHAT WORKS

A key component to effective and persuasive joint fact finding, KPI tracking, and program review is the ability to analyze what's effective, for which students, at what cost. This type of review goes by a few names, including achievement value analysis (AVA), academic return on investment (A-ROI), or cost/benefit analysis. This is a field of study that's coming into more prominence in K–12. For deeper understanding and how-to advice, see:

- Nathan Levenson, "Academic Return on Investment," in *Smarter Budgets, Smarter Schools* (Cambridge, MA: Harvard Education Press, 2012).
- Nathan Levenson, Karla Baehr, James C. Smith, and Claire Sullivan, "Calculating Academic Return on Investment," in *Spending Money Wisely: Getting the Most from School District Budgets* (Boston: District Management Council, 2014), http://www.dmcouncil.org.
- John J-H Kim, "Boosting Performance Cost Effectively: Achievement Value Analysis," *District Management Journal* (Spring 2014), http://www.dmcouncil.org.

6

MAKE BOLD AND COMPREHENSIVE PLANS

*The Better the Budget
Is for Students, the Easier
It Can Be to Pass*

Optimism, hope, and a belief that achievement can be better in the future: this seems like exactly the attitude a new superintendent, school board member, or administrator should bring to the job. Who would want a leader who is cynical and resigned to the status quo? Like Annie singing "The sun will come out tomorrow," a can-do spirit is uplifting and inspiring. It can also, surprisingly, make winning support for student-centered budgets more difficult. This may seem counterintuitive, since enthusiasm, commitment, and optimism are also key attributes to building support for promising changes. To understand this paradox, let's set a scene typical in many districts in the United States.

A new leader is hired. She brings hope, energy, and vision to the district. During the "getting to know the district" listening and learning phase, she discovers the following:

- Reading achievement has inched up over the last few years, but still too many students don't read on grade level.
- Students who have IEPs, are learning English, or are living in poverty achieve at lower levels than other students.
- Professional development seems a bit scattershot.
- More time is desired for both students and teachers.

This is a very common situation in districts big and small, urban or suburban or rural, rich or poor alike. Not to fear, within a year or two, the new leader puts forth a plan and related budget to address one or more of these challenges. While some applaud the plans, others push back against the proposed changes. To the new leader, the opposition can look like recalcitrant staff just not willing to change. It could be easy to dismiss opponents as trying to protect jobs, preserve the past, or soothe hurt pride.

LISTEN CLOSELY TO THE CRITICS

I'll confess, in my early days as a district leader serving on my local school board, I often assumed those who resisted change (and the budgets that supported the proposed changes) were just stuck in their ways. At the time, it never dawned on me that their pushback was rational and understandable. I have learned a lot since then. One event helped change my thinking greatly.

The district leadership had proposed some smart, field-tested ideas for the next budget. This included a greater use of common formative reading assessments, more instructional coaches, and targeted professional development in math. Who could argue with these rock-solid best practices?

To win over the opposition, which consisted mostly of veteran teachers, the district leaders shared their theories of action, their research base, and examples from other districts where these actions had raised achievement. They also highlighted that our reading and math results lagged behind peer communities. Clearly, change was needed, and these were thoughtful changes to address undeniable needs. Despite hours and weeks of discussion and explanation, the staff responded with petitions, raised voices, and resistance. The district persuaded few veteran staff to support the shifts in funds needed to implement these improvements.

Fortunately, the majority of the school board supported the changes and despite the stiff opposition they passed the reform budget. Sure, the reforms caused some pain—slightly larger classes, fewer new computers, and less outside PD—but it was well worth the trade-off. It took me three years to realize that the teachers who opposed the changes were the thoughtful and reasonable ones.

Mistakenly, I had viewed the staff opposition as them rejecting the new ideas, but in fact they also saw the need to improve; they just sincerely didn't believe that these changes would lead to gains for students—and here is the key point—because they believed these efforts would be poorly implemented. Why suffer the pain for no benefit, they figured.

When the school board and district leaders tried to persuade the staff that these changes were needed and prudent, and while the staff outwardly rebutted the details of the proposed changes, their inner monologue was "They will screw this up and nothing good will come from it. In all likelihood it will be a step backward, not forward." They thought this, but didn't say it out of respect and professionalism.

Over the next few years, reading assessments were implemented, but no time in the schedule was ever carved out to review the data (the assistant principals couldn't figure out how to revamp the schedule). The data was old before it was shared with staff (no one was assigned to process the results quickly), the instructional coaches hired were energetic but ineffective (favoring writing curriculum that sat on a shelf unused over working with teachers), and the math PD was scattered, "sit and git" sessions that seemed to please no one.

How did the staff know that these thoughtful plans would be implemented ineffectively? Did they have a crystal ball? A few years after passing this reform-minded budget, and with my tail between my legs, I met with the staff that led the opposition and apologized for forcing changes that amounted to nothing for kids, but brought much aggravation to teachers. They shared that they had "seen this before" and that I was "just naïve and inexperienced." They knew (and I didn't) that over the last twenty years there had been five new reading efforts, more than a dozen new approaches to PD, and a near-perfect track record of new positions being created but then unsupervised. In all, lots of new efforts and disruptions had been implemented, but the needle on student performance hadn't budged.

The irony, of course, is that this lack of past improvement fueled the desire for the reform-minded budget, but it was exactly the same lack of improvement that fueled their opposition!

I learned three lessons from this experience:

1. Veteran staff in many districts have seen lots of big ideas result in little benefit. Some resistance to supporting the next new thing is reasonable, given their experience.

2. Effective implementation matters a lot, both in the effort to actually help students but also to win support for any proposed new effort.

3. Arguing the merits of an idea is insufficient. Being convincing that the idea will be implemented well is just as important.

Over the next ten years, working with dozens of districts, I have deduced a fourth lesson, maybe the most counterintuitive:

4. Compromising in an effort to reduce pushback can make it less likely that the effort will be implemented well, and thus *increase* pushback to this particular change and all future changes. I call this the "compromise trap."

AVOID THE COMPROMISE TRAP

The vicious cycle of the compromise trap works as follows: A thoughtful plan is devised to address a real need. It will ask many to do much differently. How else can important, long-standing challenges be met? Asking few to change a little seldom leads to dramatic gains. This bold, thoughtful plan is reflected in the draft budget—cuts in some areas to fund a staff increase in another, dollars for new materials, related training, and an administrator to oversee the effort, for example.

The inevitable pushback begins. At this point, bad things can start to happen, in the name of doing good. The department losing positions attacks the need or merits of the plan. School boards and unions are uncomfortable with spending precious dollars on out-of-state training and new administrators, wishing to keep money in the classrooms. Wanting to move forward, and mindful of the pushback, the district leaders modify the plan to win support. A few "reasonable" changes are made:

- Rather than a new administrative position being created, program responsibility will be added to the plate of an existing administrator.
- Rather than most staff being sent to extensive training by the program provider, just a few will attend, and upon their return they will train their colleagues.
- Rather than the new teaching positions being filled with staff hired from open postings with the required skills and training, the teachers slated for cuts will be allowed to fill the new roles.

With a sense of some satisfaction that a compromise was forged, and with the comfort that half a loaf is better than none, the budget is passed, heralding the new program's arrival next September.

By November, the shortcomings of the spring become apparent. The administrator with the added responsibilities devoted limited time to the rollout, since he was already very busy. As a result, many of the materials didn't arrive in time for the staff to review over the summer. Some books didn't arrive until late October. The "train the trainer" staff returned from their conference upbeat, but not expert. They struggle to answer many nagging logistical questions, like how to find time, how to integrate with existing materials, and how to modify for ELL and students with special needs. At year's end, most dishearteningly, student achievement hasn't budged. One cynical soul remarks, "Why did we really expect big changes? We took the same people and gave them new roles and no training. Was this really worth the angst, energy, and money?" To be sure, not every district or program follows this path, but many do.

I have witnessed smart, bold leaders make compromises that at the time seemed artful and wise, but in hindsight undermined the success and bred reluctance by others to embrace future changes. Some deadly compromises include the following:

- Appointing a program director who despised the new program and wished it to fail
- Filling instructional coaching positions, the key implementers of the initiative, with the weakest teachers in the school to "get them out of the classroom"
- Forgoing virtually all training in the new program
- Hiring the very same teachers who had been unsuccessful in the past, but giving them a new title and two days' training
- Cutting staffing levels for the new effort by 50 percent but not scaling back the number of schools or students served

No surprise: these changes eliminated any chance of success even though they smoothed the way for approval of the budget containing the new efforts. When staff complain that the new program won't work, they may have history on their side. Knowing that staff has legitimate concerns is the first step toward winning them over. Four strategies can help convert "we have been disappointed before" opponents into strong supports:

1. Acknowledge past shortcomings
2. Build bold, comprehensive plans

3. Pilot, measure, and expand
4. Minimize "Big Idea" churn

ACKNOWLEDGE PAST SHORTCOMINGS

Nothing helps build trust more than speaking the truth. While obvious, this can be hard to do in a public setting like K–12. A new superintendent shared with me his surprise that his new plans had such limited support from teachers. After holding focus groups with teachers we learned that the last four major initiatives over ten years had all been poorly managed, they were logistical nightmares, the promised training never materialized, and the efforts dropped in a year or two. This had happened before his time, but it was front and center in the minds of many teachers. In a series of small meetings and carefully worded announcements, the superintendent shared that he had learned much from the lessons of past rollouts in the district. This helped staff at least listen to his plans. They were comforted that the superintendent had acknowledged there was a problem that needed to be solved.

Acknowledging that some past efforts have failed can be an important first step in winning support, but political savvy and careful wording is needed, especially if the less-than-stellar coaches still work in the district, or the architect of the not-very-useful curriculum is still in your cabinet. Acknowledging that we have "learned some lessons about the key skills of who makes a great coach or the attributes of an effective curriculum" sends an important message, but in a respectful way.

Taking the blame yourself can also work. One superintendent declared, "We are better at making plans than implementing them. I've come to appreciate just how complex implementation really is." This actually instilled confidence because everyone in the district already knew it to be true, and they were gladdened to know the superintendent also knew it.

BUILD BOLD, COMPREHENSIVE PLANS

Admitting shortcomings of the past is a helpful first step in winning the support of veteran staff, but it still is no guarantee that the district won't repeat similar (or new) challenges with implementation.

Often, in an effort to win broader support, districts water down or cut back some key elements of their plans. Compromise is most often seen as a virtue. It shows we are listening and responding to our critics. Unfortunately, it also often undermines the plan to the point that it won't actually raise achievement, reduce dropouts, or produce whatever the intended outcome. Those who initially favored the change lose much of their vigor when they realize a recently proposed compromise will gut the impact of the effort.

In one district, a bold effort to expand and strengthen math and English support for struggling middle school students was running into headwinds. The new program would require all intervention teachers to have deep content expertise and attend weekly planning sessions with core math and English teachers. More than half the existing staff teaching these courses didn't meet the criteria of strong content expertise, thus the pushback. As a compromise, all existing teachers would be grandfathered into these courses. That won the support (or at least ended the opposition) from the middle school staff. It also sank the spirits of the building principal, who no longer thought it was worth the effort to redesign the entire school schedule to create the common planning time, just to get the wrong people in a room every week. Even the math and English department heads lent only lukewarm support, not wanting to squander political capital on a plan that wouldn't bring about big gains.

A well-articulated, comprehensive plan can strengthen supporters and overcome the opponents. One superintendent won support and raised student achievement for a sweeping realignment of spending by steadfastly holding on to the key components of his reform, while compromising only on noncritical elements. The district wanted to invest nearly $3 million in new secondary reading teachers, curriculum, and assessments. This meant cutting $3 million (mostly in staff) to afford the new positions. To make a hard fight even harder, he wanted to change the schedules of many schools as part of the plan.

When outlining the plan as part of an early budget presentation, the superintendent declared a list of key success factors and related non-negotiables. He was explicit about all the elements that were needed for success. They included having teachers with specific training in teaching adolescents reading, extensive data and assessment to track progress, and daily common planning time, among other requirements.

As the inevitable pushback started, a wave of compromises was suggested: "let's use our existing curriculum" (which lacked the needed assessments), "let's repurpose existing staff" (who lacked the needed skills), "let's provide the program one day a week, not five." Since these were all clearly at odds with the non-negotiables, the superintendent didn't budge. His holding firm energized the middle school principals into believing that this effort would be different from the past half-hearted ones. They, in turn, agreed to a common bell schedule across all four middle schools, which provided districtwide common planning time for all the new reading teachers, a first for the district. The commitment by four principals to a common schedule was nothing short of miraculous, a fact not lost on the school board. They, in turn, strengthened their resolve to fund all the non-negotiables.

In the end, there was a compromise, but not on the key elements. The implementation was phased over a few years such that all sixth and ninth graders, but not the other grades, were served in year one. This minimized the impact on staff in year one, but didn't water down the program quality at all.

Having watched dozens, perhaps hundreds, of superintendents and school boards navigate tough budget decisions, I have seen that one fatal compromise can undermine the value of the entire effort, erode support, and sap the energy from future efforts. In school improvement, half a loaf is seldom better than none. Waiting a year to build the needed support for a comprehensive plan may be wiser than "taking what you can get."

An important corollary to the idea that people will support a comprehensive plan is that there is much value to *proving* in advance that the plan is, in fact, comprehensive. The easiest way to prove, rather than just state, comprehensiveness is to share many of the key implementation decisions at the same time that the plan itself is announced. This might include who will lead the effort, what materials and training will be provided, or how the staff involved will be selected.

Continuing with the secondary reading example, the superintendent announced, right at the start, who would lead the effort (a well-respected rising star in the district), who would teach (this would be determined through a competitive process open to people outside the district, with no grandfathered protections), the hiring process (there would be a new job description, so there'd be no bumping of less capable staff into the role), and so on. Making and sharing these decisions helped further convince key stakeholders that this was a plan worth fighting for.

Had the superintendent said he would pick a leader and set the hiring criteria after the plan was approved, many would-be supporters might have reasonably worried that political favoritism or collective bargaining rules would undermine the effort and reduce their zeal to offer strong support.

PILOT, MEASURE, AND EXPAND

Communicating a bold, comprehensive plan helps win support, but these are still just promises. Veteran staff have seen many a sincere promise devolve into a watered-down, ineffective plan. Actual success can help sway even the most ardent critic. Thus, the third way to convince key stakeholders that a plan is comprehensive and will in fact help kids is to pilot the plan and prove it works.

Some districts have won support for big changes by starting small. They pilot the program to prove its worth. Key to this strategy, however, is that the pilot must be carefully and objectively measured for effectiveness. Since pilots typically start with the advocates, simply declaring a year later that the early adopters were pleased seldom convinces the critics. Rigorous comparative student growth data is critical to proving whether the pilot was successful.

Pilots, however, have a downside. When a plan is rolled out in just a few rooms, grades, or schools, it may be doomed to failure because the pilot can't be a comprehensive plan. Schedules aren't changed, or the right staff aren't hired, or critical supports aren't put in place. The same list of non-negotiables applies to any pilot. Sometimes only a large-scale implementation is possible if it's to be done right.

MINIMIZE "BIG IDEA" CHURN

By definition, veteran staff have been around for years. They have seen many plans, even great ones, washed away by a new superintendent, chief academic officer, or school boards. Even my own wife sided against me, expressing sympathy for my staff. "You come in with big ideas, sweeping changes, and while they are good ideas (*what else could she say?*), won't the next superintendent undo your plans? You won't stay forever; teachers and principals will outlast you."

New leaders want to make their mark. New leaders lean toward what they know or what worked for them elsewhere. New leaders are often hired to make things better, so it seems logical that moving away from the status quo will be needed. Without change, how can things change for the better? This reasonable penchant for change by new leaders, when viewed from the vantage point of veteran staff, looks like a fast-spinning carousel—lots of colors and noise, but mostly a blur that won't lead anywhere but back to the same old place once the music stops. Perhaps the most cynical expression I hear in districts across the country is the quietly muttered "This too shall pass."

Fortunately, an endless flow of new good ideas isn't necessary to help students. Many of the most improved districts stick with the same plan for years, even decades. A review, for example, of Broad Prize-winning districts—large urban districts that improved faster than their peers—reveals that these top-performing districts typically have had very stable strategies carried out by a succession of superintendents or long-serving superintendents with a steady hand. Knowing that a plan will last and be fine-tuned, rather than abandoned with the next new hire, fad, or gust of wind, can also reduce stakeholder opposition.

While we can empathize with the initiative fatigue of many adults, kids still need most districts to improve, so what to do?

- *Acknowledge past churn.* Staff will appreciate an honest assessment of prior fleeting reforms. Simply by listing and noting that some efforts have come and gone quickly, leaders send a message that they're aware of this pitfall, and thus might be less likely to repeat it.
- *Build off of existing efforts.* Improving or slightly redirecting existing efforts can help ease pushback. This creates a sense of fine-tuning (a good thing) versus abandoning for the sake of change (a bad thing) or layering the new on top of the old (a worse thing). One district, wanting to amp up the use of data by teachers, originally proposed hiring data coaches, setting aside time before school for data meetings, and hiring a director of data use. This seemed like a heavy added load to the staff, and disrespectful of their relatively new and appreciated professional learning community (PLC) meetings held during the school day. Teachers pushed back on the proposal, which also undercut principal support.

  A better plan could have honored and acknowledged the past, saved some money, and reduced pushback. The data initiative could have been integrated into the ongoing PLC effort. Existing meetings could include a much heavier dose of looking at data and formulating what to do based on the data. Existing coaches could have been screened; many had the skills to lead data-driven planning.

- *Wait to finish what was already started.* Sometimes going slow will speed up getting to the finish line. As a new superintendent, I was convinced focusing on elementary reading was the key to closing our achievement gap for students of color or with special needs. I planned on rolling out a major new initiative, which included lots of disruptions to past spending to pay for curriculum, classroom libraries, instructional coaches, and reading teachers. Having been hired explicitly as a change agent, I thought little of starting a new, major initiative on day one. I was not surprised that many staff negatively impacted by such a plan fought the change, but was dismayed at how many likely supporters seemed to be providing halfhearted support. Turns out, the district was halfway through implementing a new elementary writing effort, which it didn't want to abandon.

  I was surprised that the district had chosen to focus first on writing, but a forceful ELA director (and former English teacher) loved writing and didn't have the same passion for reading. I thought this was the wrong focus, but not a terrible one. I decided to wait a year before rolling out the new reading effort. I messaged clearly that we would focus on elementary writing for one more year, then shift to reading. This greatly increased the support for sweeping changes to our reading program and dramatic shifts to the budget.

- *Look for an existing, worthwhile focus.* The temptation to start a new, high-profile effort is strong, especially by new leaders. In a district with a history of stopping and starting initiatives on a regular basis, rather than planning from scratch, it can be easier to select an existing effort and improve and expand it.

I have seen a few savvy new superintendents conduct a thorough review of recent efforts, and choose among them where to focus limited dollars, hours, and political capital rather than build a plan from scratch. This isn't as flashy or headline making as big, bold, new reforms, but it can ease the way to shifting resources and helping students.

- *Use sustainable funding sources.* One of the most common reasons districts pull the plug on new efforts is that they were funded by grants or other one-time dollars. When these funds run out, the effort ends, even if it's working well or showing promise.

  There is a paradox here. Many leaders purposely use one-time dollars or grants to *gain* support for new efforts. This approach often eliminates some of the hard decisions like reducing staffing in one area to pay for new staff in another, such as fewer paraprofessionals to fund more certified reading teachers. Using a grant can reduce (for the moment) the unpleasant task of laying off some paraprofessionals. While this makes it easy on the paras and their supporters, many a savvy staff member realizes that the new reading teachers will likely last only as long as the grant. Some districts make the tough choices up front to free up the operating budget, while others go so far as dedicating a specific bond or ongoing funding stream to a particular effort.

In the long run, a sustained focus on a few key, coherent comprehensive strategies will raise achievement and also make budgeting easier. Sticking to a plan and then refining and improving it will allow the district to implement well and minimize the disruptions caused by each new budget.

7

CRAFT MESSAGES THAT RESONATE WITH STAKEHOLDERS

How You Talk About Spending Decisions Can Sway or Discourage Support

"Why don't they get it?"

I often hear this phrase muttered in frustration toward the end of the budget cycle. Annoyance, anger, disappointment—all rolled up into five short words. "It" refers to the district's thoughtful budget proposals, and "they" is everyone not supporting the budget shifts, cuts, and additions.

When I debrief with superintendents the morning after a watered-down, compromise-laden budget was passed, much energy in the conversation focuses on the people who opposed the budget, but there is often little reflection as to why more people didn't support the efforts. A very common theme in these sad Monday morning quarterbacking sessions is how few people understood the why and the what, and how often misinformation was more widespread than the truth.

At the end of the day, smart budgets pass because enough people want them to pass. Prior chapters outlined all the legitimate reasons smart, caring people will oppose smart, caring, student-centered budgets, especially during tight fiscal times when new efforts to help raise achievement must come at the cost of ending something else. If it's a given that people who are negatively impacted will push back, then it's critical that district leaders actively and effectively build support not only internally but externally with other key stakeholders, including the board, community, city and town officials, parents, teachers not directly impacted, administrators, and even students. Since no district leader can sit down for coffee with every stakeholder to walk through the proposed budget, larger-scale communication efforts are central to winning support for shifting resources.

CRAFT MORE COMPELLING MESSAGES

The first obstacle in developing an effective communication strategy to pass smart budgets is believing that better communications matter, and the second obstacle is believing that your district in particular needs a new, more effective communication strategy.

In years past, some teachers lamented, "I taught it, but they didn't learn it." Integral to the statement was the idea that I, as a teacher, did my part, but the student didn't do his share. The problem rested squarely on the learner, not the teacher. Today we recognize that the teacher shares much responsibility for a student's lack of learning. The teacher is expected to change her approach, supplement, and try new strategies until the student learns.

Some districts, in like fashion, bemoan that they built a wise and thoughtful budget but stakeholders didn't support it. Just as the unsuccessful teacher tried hard, worked long hours, and followed a well-worn path, district leaders do try to garner support for their budgets, but are often not as successful as desired or needed.

It seems that, too often, district leaders feel that the facts will speak for themselves, and thus simply sharing the budget plan should generate sufficient support. I certainly fell into this trap many times. Our inner monologue might include "State revenue is down 10 percent, so of course people know cuts are required," or "Personalized learning is key to meeting each child's needs and new handheld technology is the foundation of personalized learning, so cuts are needed to fund these purchases." These are simple messages with clear, easy-to-understand logic. Shouldn't that be enough? It's not.

As funds become ever more scarce and budgets harder to balance, more district leaders are more proactively engaging in budget-related communication strategies. Unfortunately, too often they aren't all that effective, since most district leaders I know feel they could do more good for their students, despite limited resources, if they could just get the support to move more dollars around. The difficulty of winning support is so omnipresent that most district leaders I know self-censor—never even proposing spending options (usually cuts) that they believe in because they doubt the ideas will be supported. This thinking treats stakeholder support as fixed—"it is what it is"—rather than something that can be managed and increased.

At this point you might be thinking, "Yes, communication is key; I know that." Great, but is your district good at communicating these tough and complex messages? Many superintendents, school boards, and other leaders seem to give themselves fairly high marks. A large-scale experiment in strategic budgeting serves as a cautionary note. Recently a foundation offered significant consulting support to a number of districts attempting wholesale changes in how they use their resources. These districts readily and hungrily sought help with all matters related to the technical and analytical parts of freeing up funds, but opted out from much help with communications and outreach. Puzzled by this dichotomy—yes to number-crunching support but no to communications help— the foundation wondered if the diverse group of firms offering the help lacked or were perceived to be lacking expertise in winning over supporters and influencing others. The foundation upped its offer. It would provide, free to the districts, consulting and hands-on support from the well-respected organizations that specialized in K–12 and nonprofit communications. Still not much interest. Even as a few of the districts ran into significant stakeholder backlash, bad press, and a rampant rumor mill, the districts saw limited need for help. "We've got this covered," they shared.

From the outside looking in, the need for a very different approach to communicating with stakeholders seems significant. One of the top recommendations from a 2014 convening of school finance experts from around the country—people who collectively have observed many hundreds of budget battles—was for districts to dramatically improve their communications strategies. There seems to be a disconnect between what others see and what districts observe when they look in the mirror. Perhaps districts are slow to see the need for wholesale communication changes because they were actually quite skilled at an approach that worked well for many years, but in a different context. Most districts routinely passed budgets every year, and often with minimal aggravation. They had an approach that worked just fine.

But the world has changed. Districts now face years of needs and costs rising faster than revenue, as previously discussed.

The approaches that worked well in the past won't be as successful in this new reality. Many district budgets moved forward smoothly and, in pursuit of better outcomes, added new efforts funded by new dollars on top of old efforts and old spending. These budgets avoided the painful, pushback-provoking cuts and resource shifts so common in the new era. When cuts were needed in the past, they often focused on postponable costs, like capital projects and textbooks, or stayed far away from teachers, concentrating on central office, outside contractors, or extracurriculars. Often, districts expected to get the needed funds in future years and restore these temporary cuts. New times, however, call for new strategies. Doing better by kids will typically mean shifting funds from popular programs and negatively impacting some staff. New times call for a new message, delivered in new ways.

Develop the Framing, Not Just the Message

How district leaders talk about money—the *framing* and *messaging*, in the jargon of the field—is an emerging science. After a set of resource decisions is made, how the recommendations are framed—the context created and the reasons provided—can make a world of difference. Effective framing and messaging can increase the chance that more funds will be provided; build support for difficult, student-centered shifts in resources; and make staff feel good about their work and prospects for success—or not. Given the same budget decisions, very different stakeholder reactions are possible based on the framing and messaging.

It's shocking how powerful framing can be. Growing up, my siblings and I hated losing power during a storm. Dinner was subpar, it got cold in the house, and life got boring very fast. We all waited anxiously and seemingly forever for the power to return. Like cutting a budget, there is nothing good in a black-out. Outside forces beyond our control made us suffer a bit.

My children's experience with blackouts, thanks to my wife's clever framing, was very different, even though as part of the wired generation raised with YouTube, Xbox, and Wi-Fi they seemed even more likely to hate a power outage.

Rather than frame a power outage as a loss, my wife explained it's an opportunity to do things we wouldn't normally do. This included eating cereal for dinner, playing cards by candlelight, sleeping on the floor in mom and dad's room, and donning our blackout sweatshirts. When the lights did come back on, my kids often asked if we could turn off the lights so the blackout could continue. This is a perfect example of helping others to see the silver lining in an otherwise undesirable situation.

Create the Right Context: It's About Helping Kids, Not Balancing a Budget

While the driving goal of student-centric, difficult-decision-laden budgets is helping all kids learn, this message is often the first to be jettisoned during budget discussions in tough financial times. Too often the budget conversation is about numbers, not kids.

The first best practice for effective communication about resources is to be sure that the proposed budget actually is about helping more students learn more. There is no magic phrase that can generate broad support for a budget that is just credits and debits in balance. When a bold, comprehensive, and coherent plan drives the budget shifts, cuts, and additions, it's easier for stakeholders to actively lend their support. Thus the first step in effective communication and building support for smart budgets is shifting the budget, in the mind of stakeholders, from a financial document to a statement of priorities and a plan for raising achievement.

Money is not the exciting part of education; kids learning and excelling is. When the budget is just numbers, it's a chore. When the budget is an annual battle between the schools and tight-fisted finance committees, taxpayers, and the state, it's a power struggle—one likely to be lost. When the budget is viewed primarily as an employment roster, it becomes very personal about who stays and who goes. But when the budget is consistently discussed as the blueprint for helping students be successful, more stakeholders will be positively engaged and the reasons for swallowing some tough medicine are never absent from the discussion.

Too often, likely supporters stay silent while the negatively impacted staff mount strong resistance, because when the budget is framed as a financial document, few stakeholders feel motivated to engage. The more clearly the budget is an education plan for kids, the more supporters become *real* supporters.

Thus every budget discussion, presentation, and document must open with a clear statement of educational priorities, a well-articulated theory of action for raising achievement, and inspiration for helping students. The specifics of spending and shifting should be tied explicitly to these educational priorities. Effective budget presentations needn't have a single number for the first fifteen PowerPoint slides or twenty minutes of talking. The plan and the vision need to be well established first and every time.

Sometimes, however, even when the budget does embody a clear vision and comprehensive learning strategies, this compelling message is lost in the din of financial talk. Sometimes when an educationally strong budget is presented, the vision is relegated to a footnote, figuratively speaking. Budget documents and public presentations may include the district's vision statement, but not actually outline in detail the district's theory of action and how every addition or subtraction, or change in the budget, is connected to the vision. Strategic plans typically explain the why and the how, but budget documents often open with an accounting of revenue and expenses, such as "Cost will increase by 5 percent and revenue will only increase by 2 percent; thus, we have a gap of 3 percent." True, but not inspiring.

Again, in practice this means budget PowerPoint presentations might have fifteen slides outlining the district's teaching and learning plan, before the first financial figure is shared. It means the actual budget document should look a lot like a strategic plan, with as many pages devoted to why we are doing things and how they will help children, as to how much we are going to spend on what. Leaders adept at winning support for student-centered budgets spend the first fifteen or twenty minutes of every budget discussion outlining the theory of action, the need for change, and a "can do, will do" plan for helping more kids learn more—all before sharing a single financial figure.

WALK IN THE SHOES OF TEACHERS AND TAXPAYERS, NOT JUST STUDENTS

It's much easier to create inspiration and support for a budget that is a strong educational plan, but effective framing of budget messages also requires district leaders to view the situation from the vantage point of the listener. Helping kids learn is important, but it is not the only concern for staff and community members.

Some district leaders have a tendency to set the context as it looks from their vantage point. When talking to teachers, principals, and others, they explain the outside constraints they face as district leaders, such as state mandates, rising pension costs, state accountability sanctions, shrinking enrollment, and dropping property values. While these are harsh realities for district leaders, and the reason they must make decisions that are tough on staff, these are not the pressing concerns of most listeners.

When the budget message starts with an honest recap of the listener's reality, teachers and the public become less defensive or oppositional because they know the speaker is aware of their situation and has, hopefully, factored it into the plan. Too often staff or taxpayers dismiss tough messages because they feel leaders are "out of touch." The acknowledgment that staff are being asked to do more sheltered English immersion, adapt to the Common Core, and so on, and that these changes will be hard on them, actually helps them support (or object less to) what follows. They are comforted to know that the proposals are built on an accurate understanding of their reality. Critically important, however, is that the decisions in the budget must actually take into account staff realities. This is another way in which comprehensive plans win support and piecemeal decisions draw wrath.

Acknowledge Staff Realities

Adding new assessments and the tools and staff to use them well is a great example of how an honest recounting from the teachers' perspective can win support. It's surprising, at first glance, how little staff often support funding new benchmarking assessments, and the people and time to make use of them. In the age of data-driven decision making, shouldn't one be a bit embarrassed to be "antidata"? When we look at the situation from the teachers' vantage point, however, the seemingly strong educational message "We need the new assessment system to identify each student's individual needs and provide personalized intervention" is much less compelling if current benchmark assessments are only marginally aligned to the pacing guides, and results are returned to teachers six to eight weeks after the fact, which is too late to be useful. A message that begins, "I know we have challenges with our current assessment system, especially alignment to the curriculum, and slow processing of the results, but this new system will address these shortcomings by . . ." will be much better received.

The irony is that it was exactly these shortcomings that prompted the desire for the new benchmark systems, tools, and staff, but a reluctance to publicly discuss current problems undermines support from staff and principals who worry that the new efforts will be no more effective than the past, so why suffer to get the new.

Walking in the shoes of teachers may be a bit humbling at times, but as educators we shouldn't find it too hard to understand where they are coming from. Getting inside the heads of some community members may be a bit trickier.

Appreciate the Community's Financial Norms

"Like people from another planet," blurted the local power broker in my former district during a budget planning session. Who was this alien presenting to the town's finance committee? It was a well-meaning, financially savvy CFO. Smart and experienced, the district business manager struggled to connect with the people who had much sway over the district's budget. The points of contention were many, including health insurance rates, sick time, and technology spending. Time and time again, the CFO rebuffed suggestions by the appointed finance board as crazy, unethical, or outright illegal. Such outlandish ideas included:

- health insurance copays of $25 per doctor visit;
- not carrying over unused sick days into the next year; and
- teachers' learning new software on their own, without formal training.

What the CFO didn't realize, and couldn't believe, was that these unreasonable, inconvenient ideas were long the norm in the private sector, where all eight committee members worked day in and day out.

To be sure, schools aren't businesses and many private sector practices are undesirable or untenable in a K–12 setting. That's not the point. The point is that what's typical in K–12 can seem unreasonable to others. Just as visiting a foreign country and not knowing the local customs can lead to much unintended disrespect, so can communicating about budgets to the broader public without an appreciation for what's normal in their world.

Having worked in both worlds, I'm often struck not just by how different the financial norms are in K–12 compared to the private sector, but by how little each universe seems to know of the other. On more than a few occasions I have asked school and district leaders to take a quick quiz called "Do you feel uncomfortable?" They are asked to rate their comfort level with a number of potential resource reallocation options. What I don't tell the educators is that each decision to be considered is commonplace in well-run, "great place to work" private companies. Typically educators rate at least a few of these private sector everyday realities as unethical, with the strongest level of distaste for:

- employees paying 30 percent of health insurance premiums and having a $1,000 deductible;
- paying more effective people more;

- not paying for unused sick days;
- suddenly, involuntarily transferring employees as needs shift in the organization; and
- not providing pensions to new employees.

The suggestion isn't that districts should adopt any of these private sector practices, but that it's important to know the reality of key stakeholders, especially when discussing benefits, raises, and job security. This requires taking some time and asking and listening to community members to learn about their financial realities before sharing the district's. It also means that it's important to share what's typical in K–12 so that the public doesn't perceive the commonplace as over the top.

Demonstrate and Communicate Frugal Stewardship of Taxpayer Dollars

One of the most compelling messages that can win over supporters but is seldom stressed—and worse, its absence actually diminishes support—is that the district has been and will be a frugal steward of taxpayers' money. In many focus groups and surveys, taxpayers, including parents, often express that even if the vision is clear and compelling, even if the dollars will help children (even their children), and even if there is a budget gap, their support for a district budget, especially an increase, requires a strong sense that past dollars were well spent and future spending won't be wasted. Their inner monologue goes something like this, "Sure, we do need more _____, and it's terrible that the state cut _____, but if the district didn't waste money on _____, then it could afford _____."

Perhaps this crucial message is missing from many public-facing budget discussions because district leaders take it for granted that they are already perceived as frugal stewards of taxpayer dollars—because they are! In my experience reviewing hundreds of district budgets and in conversations with many hundreds of superintendents, I have found that nearly all hold fiscal stewardship as a core value. They agonize over spending money as if it were their own. As finances have been tight for years, most districts are well past funding nice-to-haves and have long focused on managing every taxpayer dollar like it's a rare commodity. For many leaders, the view from the inside is "We are excellent fiscal stewards, and no one could question this."

Unfortunately, the view from the outside can be very different, even if misinformed. In silence, false perceptions take root. In some of the most well-managed, fiscally conservative districts, distrust and concerns over wasteful spending abound. Striking examples include the following:

- One district was considered a reckless spender for buying a fancy central office building, even though it was a sublease that saved 20 percent over its previous lease.
- Another district was lambasted and punished for the fancy marble entranceway to the central office, even though it purchased a bankrupt factory for cents on the dollar to expand a very popular vocational program and then sold off the old central office to move into empty space in the new tech school.
- One (a lot more than one) district was pilloried for its year-over-year increases in spending, but few realized enrollment was growing rapidly, much faster than spending.
- Yet another misunderstood frugal district lost some public confidence by adding a central-office cost containment specialist—a position that saved many times the specialist's salary.

In all these cases, a wise and prudent decision was viewed by many as playing loose with taxpayer money. The crux of the problem was that these decisions were "seen," but not heard. In all of these examples, communication was limited. The decisions and related facts were discussed at school board meetings, but not directly addressed months or years later when future budgets were presented. Few people listened or remembered the first conversations. They needed to be reminded often.

What's especially notable about the preceding list of misinterpreted acts of frugality is that they all relate to the central office. Parents and taxpayers love small classes and small central offices. While both aren't supported by the research, they remain popular. Central office spending is often the most visible barometer of frugality.

So what to do about helping the public appreciate and believe that their dollars are being spent well?

- *Explain big purchases, again and again.* Every budget presentation should include a recap of major purchases over time, including the rationale and financial benefits. Even five years after the district office moved into the "marble-clad palace" (aka a bankrupt building that expanded a key service at a bargain price and saved on rent), parents and taxpayers needed to be reminded just how wise of an investment this was.
- *Don't let internal accounting inflate central office spending.* Despite the public's disdain for central office spending, many district budgets massively overreport how much is spent on central office staff. For example, ELL teachers, special education staff, professional development, instruction coaches, busing, and other expenses that serve students and schools are often listed on budget

documents as "central office," not as school expenses. One large district officially reports that 50 percent of spending is in the central office budget, when in fact what the public considers central office (administrators, back office functions like payroll and HR) was less than 10 percent.

- *Remind everyone of past cuts.* When tough decisions were made a year or two ago, they feel like fresh wounds to district leaders, but are often distant memories for the public. Budget presentations should catalogue prior tough board decisions to remind everyone of its history of managing funds well.

- *In growing districts, shift the focus to per-pupil spending.* As enrollment rises, so do costs. More kids mean more teachers, textbooks, and so on. The public can't easily gauge that a 10 percent increase in spending over time, driven by a 10 percent increase in enrollment, really isn't runaway spending, but actually strong fiscal restraint. Sharing that per-pupil spending has remained flat clearly communicates strong stewardship of taxpayer dollars.

- *Abandon what doesn't work.* The surest sign of fiscal trustworthiness is to stop spending on programs that don't produce results. Ending programs because they are ineffective, and saying so publicly, builds trust that future dollars will be put to good use.

- *Proclaim what you didn't spend.* An often-overlooked way to prove fiscal restraint is to highlight what you don't spend. Few budgets have a page that lists what's not in the budget, but it's still important for the public to know what you don't fund. External benchmarking, often done by an objective third party, can highlight that the district is spending less on $x, y,$ or z than like communities.

This can be very impactful. Knowing that the district is running lean, compared to like districts, can prove to the public that the district leaders are being frugal with taxpayer dollars.

Highlighting services that the district gets for free (or at greatly reduced costs) also instills a sense of prudent fiscal stewardship. This can include partnerships with nonprofits for mental health or drug and alcohol counseling, school resource officers paid by the police budget, or large grants subsidizing major initiatives.

- *Ask, listen, research, and respond.* Perhaps the most powerful, yet time-consuming, strategy to prove each dollar entrusted to the district is going to a good use is to ask the public what they see as unnecessary or wasteful, and respond in a methodical, nondefensive way. Online surveys or links on the district's website are a low-cost way to find out what people think is wasteful. There are a few variations on this idea, but they all have some key elements in common.

  It starts with the ask. Soliciting ideas for how the district could save money is a surefire way to know what's perceived as not a good use of taxpayer dollars. Getting a long list is easy. The next step, listening, can be the hardest. The desire to correct misconceptions and defend past decisions can be overwhelming. A quick response, however, is often viewed as defensive and a sign of not really being interested in new ideas. Listening and acknowledging, but not responding, is critical. People must feel heard (and actually *be* heard).

  Before responding, conduct formal research. For example, when out-of-state travel is criticized as excessive and unneeded, don't answer (even though it's true),

"Out-of-state travel is minimal and would have only a tiny impact on the budget," but rather get the details. This is the step that makes the strategy time-consuming, but it is key to gaining and retaining credibility. Sharing that out-of-state travel totaled $12,450, that $10,000 of this was paid by an outside foundation, and that the balance was spent for teachers to learn how to use a new set of science tools is a more trust-building response.

Finally, share the response in writing and publicly. If one person raised the issue, it's likely many more are thinking the same. Listing both the question and the answer on the district website is one way of sharing the response. If a particular idea is raised repeatedly, a dedicated letter, e-mail, public presentation, and/or inclusion in the next budget presentation might make sense.

DON'T UNDERMINE YOUR MESSAGE

There is no shortage of ideas for how to prove the leadership's concern for taxpayer dollars, but there are a few common messages that can undermine this trust.

Blaming unfunded mandates for spending increases can feel like weak stewardship to some. New requirements from the state or feds—such as new curriculum standards like Common Core or new required services, such as Applied Behavior Analysis (ABA) for students with autism—definitely raise costs and pressure budgets. The need is real, but the message "We need more money because of these new mandates" often fails to resonate with the public. The unspoken implication of this statement is "Since we must do more, we need more money because there is nothing we currently do that we should stop doing." This angers many taxpayers. When a taxpayer's car breaks down, he too has an unplanned expense, but he doesn't ask his employer for a raise. He makes trade-offs, such as eating out less or shortening a planned vacation.

Build and Maintain Trust

Every district leader I have ever met values and knows how important it is to be trustworthy. While the importance is universally understood, some district leaders may not realize that they might be unintentionally undermining their credibility, which makes it hard for others to believe that tough spending choices are unavoidable. There are a few ways to avoid this accident.

DON'T CALL AN INCREASE A DECREASE. Lots of districts are cutting their budgets and even more are trimming staff, but sometimes a 2 percent *increase* is billed as a cut, undermining trust. This isn't a case of dishonesty, but district leaders often use a different definition for some key terms. For most taxpayers and finance officials, moving from a $100 million budget to a $102 million budget isn't a reduction. But from the district's perspective, if costs for existing staff and programs (such as steps, lanes, out-of-district tuitions, transportation, and health insurance) rise by, say, $5 million dollars, then $3 million in cuts to staff or services is needed despite a $2 million increase in spending.

An equally damaging variant on this is when cuts are measured against spending *requested* by schools and departments rather than against the current year. As a school board member I was dumbfounded when our superintendent declared he submitted a budget with a 5 percent total reduction, even though spending went up by a healthy dose. With calculator in hand, I searched through the budget to see what I had missed—where were the cutbacks; who was being let go? After an hour of line-by-line review I gave up and called him. Turns out, we were spending more than the current year but the plan was 5 percent less than what his cabinet requested. Needless to say, the finance committee also took umbrage with the idea that spending more was a cut.

The flip side to this is, don't lose credibility by taking credit for declining enrollment. One superintendent routinely heralded his fiscal responsibility by holding budget increases to less than inflation—on the surface, surely a sign of fiscal austerity and restraint. Unfortunately, enrollment was dropping 2 percent a year. Per-pupil spending was rising at a decent clip, and many knew this.

DON'T PROMISE THE WORLD. It can be tempting to oversell the value of new spending to win support. "Read 180 is proven to be effective, and can ensure all our students will read on grade level and can comprehend college-level text." If only this were true. Yes, when used well, it's a great product, but seldom does any one product, program, or strategy deliver miracles. People remember the big promises, and as follow-up studies are becoming more common, even decent results can look lackluster compared to grand promises. This undermines future credibility.

PLAN AHEAD WITH MULTIYEAR BUDGETING. Nearly all district budgets cover one year's spending. Single-year budgeting can undermine trust, however. For example, a district facing a deficit plans thoughtfully, makes smart cuts, and proposes a budget that does more for students and expands teacher development despite fewer dollars being available. This should engender a great deal of trust and comfort that scarce dollars are being spent wisely. That's not always the case, however. Next year the first budget presentation opens with the dreaded gap slide. The district faces a shortfall and can't bring everyone back unless more money is provided, and it wants more dollars for training again.

"Wow," thinks the public, "pretty incompetent management. Didn't we just fix the budget problem last year and spend a fortune on PD as well?" While the district leadership was painfully aware of a recurring structural deficit and a three-year phase-in plan for Common Core training, the public wasn't. Good planning can be perceived as out-of-control spending. Multiyear budgets can help change this.

Creating multiyear budgets is the norm in the private sector, but uncommon in K–12. A multiyear budget is a special kind of plan. It's typically only a few pages long and includes only large line items over the next three to five years. It might list all the major revenue streams and their forecasted levels, such as an operating budget increase of 2 percent a year (based on historical trends), reduction in state aid (end of a special grant), and more Title I due to changes in students served.

It also forecasts the district's expenses in a dozen or two major categories like classroom teachers, special education, transportation, and custodial/maintenance. Again, these are estimates based on known increases like steps and lanes or bus contracts slated to expire, plus a reasonable guess for unknown increases is also included. Finally, student enrollment is forecasted as well. In the preceding example, the public would have known that the cuts weren't a one-time occurrence, nor was the added training.

Goldilocks should be your guide to forecasting future revenue and expenses. Rosy revenue forecasts or overly conservative, "we don't know for sure, so let's call it no increase" thinking defeats the purpose. Forecasts that reflect the most likely reality are "just right."

One district took multiyear planning a step further. It forecasted five-years-out enrollment growth, reduced federal funding, and rising special ed costs, and shared an ugly reality that current tax rates would lead to ever-shrinking spending on general education students. Taxpayers in this fiscally conservative town approved an increase to cover all five years in exchange for a promise not to ask for more money during the five years. It worked so well, the district did it again years later.

Respect the Public

As with trust, all district leaders know the importance of respecting stakeholders. But in parallel fashion, they sometimes unknowingly can be perceived as disrespecting the public.

For example, motivated by a sincere belief or a bit of calculation, leaders commonly frame the budget debate, especially around the need for more money, in "pay up or children will suffer greatly" terms. "We cannot meet the most basic needs of children given the draconian cuts we are confronting." I have heard dozens of permutations on this end-of-world prediction, including (seriously): "Why doesn't everyone just start homeschooling their kids; we won't be able to provide a quality education anymore!" This messaging can work in the short run. Often, tax increases or shifts in town/city budgets help forestall the feared "end of the world" and avoid the tough budget decisions.

In today's environment this apocalyptic messaging has drawbacks. When the extra funds don't come—and more often than ever they don't—credibility is damaged because caring, smart district leaders do manage to find a way to provide a good education to children despite the cuts. When this happens, it can seem like the district was trying to scare the public, which doesn't feel respectful.

A variant on this Armageddon theme is threatening to cut positions that could have dire consequences—often paired with a heart-tugging story about the nurse who, thinking quickly, administered an EpiPen as a child's breathing became impaired, or a potential suicide prevented by high school counselors—as a means of coaxing more dollars from reluctant taxpayers. Always respectful to the children and with great sadness, the district sends a clear message: if we don't get more money, bad—very bad—things might happen to children.

While certain to motivate parents, this framing tends to alienate many others. It is often seen as a bluff. If you really thought children might die from cutting nursing hours by 10 percent, then shouldn't you reduce custodians by 10 percent instead in order to keep the nurses? When I have confronted superintendents and school board members who use this tactic, they often express the desire to shock the public out of their complacency ("They don't get it!"). Fearing that taxpayers (even parents) might support fewer custodians, they select a more disturbing alternative. Unfortunately, many stakeholders assume that the disturbing option was in fact selected in order to prod them to action.

One last reason to avoid end-of-the-world framing is that it can be very harmful to district staff. Sometimes leaders try to press a point externally and overlook the impact it can have internally. Teachers and principals follow the budget debate closely. Using apocalyptic language can have some unintended negative consequences. When staff hear from their leaders that they lack the resources to be successful, it can quickly undermine their enthusiasm for trying new approaches or keeping expectations high.

MAKE THE MESSAGE PERSONAL TO THE LISTENER

Effective messaging appeals to the head and the heart. It has a factual and personal tug. The facts detail the "what," such as "We are adding reading teachers" or "We are offering low enrollment courses at the high school every other year." These concrete plans should be born of joint fact finding, be aligned to the district's strategy and theory of action, and be bold and comprehensive. This is the stuff that appeals to the head.

The framing can help appeal to the heart. Building an emotional connection for changes in the budget might seem a tall order. Dollars, cents, line items, and revenue streams aren't the stuff of heartwarming Hallmark cards. In reality, all good resource decisions are what's best for students, so just behind the accounting is a child's future. The emotional connection is always there, but sometimes we forget to bring it to the forefront.

Some district leaders can be reluctant to wrap a sound, solid plan in a heart-tugging wrapper. Anything along these lines can feel like Madison Avenue marketing spin, and some leaders feel that's not them or it's not needed. Paradoxically, however, nearly all of the pushback to tough, student-centric budget decisions is typically built on an emotional appeal and often very effective at impeding good decisions. "Children will die" was a very effective pushback to my highly analytical study of the patterns of children walking to school in the morning. Yes, we had graphs showing zero children actually crossed the street at one-third of the locations where our crossing guards were posted. The facts were strong, but in an effort to save jobs the opponents didn't refute the walking studies, the charts, the graphs, or the data. Instead, they talked endlessly about hurt and maimed kids. And they carried the day.

Connecting the proposed changes to students, one student in particular, can help increase the emotional appeal of the message. I'm surprised by how many budget presentations start with a financial overview, then move right into cuts and additions. The first third of any budget discussion or presentation should be about how the proposed budget helps children. It wouldn't be bad to have a few images of students as well before the spreadsheets dominate.

Simply reminding stakeholders why the change is going to help students is an easy first step—for example, reminding the world that the district is adding more reading teachers because if a student can't read well by the end of third grade, her chances of graduating or having a successful career after graduating plummet. Make the connection between the student need and the pain. "We have an obligation to give every student in the district this leg up. It's unfortunate that we can't add more reading teachers without reducing the number of paraprofessionals who are currently trying to help struggling readers but haven't been effective enough."

Great communicators have long known that embodying a big idea down to a single person can be compelling. President Reagan was the first to bring average citizens to his State of the Union address and tell their story. Bill Clinton brought James Brady, the former Reagan press secretary who was injured by gunfire during the assassination attempt on President Reagan, to personalize the need for gun control. Symbolic guests needn't be famous either. A year later, Cindy Perry was sitting next to the first lady. Who is Cindy Perry? A mother of four who joined AmeriCorps to teach reading to second graders in rural Kentucky. Cindy helped remind America that AmeriCorps, a signature program for the president, wasn't about big government spending, but about real people helping real people.

Even though it's been years, I remember like yesterday one principal speaking publicly in favor a very tough budget choice to reduce the number of paraprofessionals in exchange for reading teachers. Rather than state the research or his professional judgment, he simply said, "I want to tell you about Max [not his real name]. He is a student in my school and he is more than two years behind in reading. We care deeply about him, and yet have failed him! He can't read well; this we know for certain. He gets help from a paraprofessional because we haven't enough skilled teachers to help him. The paraprofessional is a wonderful person, but she did not go to college and has no training as a teacher, let alone a reading teacher. She reads to Max and Max reads to her, but this isn't teaching him to read better. He is falling further behind each year and I fear for his future. He needs a skilled reading teacher; we owe him this."

It was as if Max were in the room, and it brought home the point better than a research paper or a data table.

Connecting the message to particular schools also helps add an emotional component to the message. Tip O'Neill, the only Speaker of the US House of Representatives to hold the leadership position for five consecutive terms, was fond of saying, "All politics is local." Even though he helped govern all fifty states, he always connected his national agenda to its local impact. For example, when O'Neill wanted to pass a $1 billion jobs bill, he publicized in detail all the benefits to the residents in the districts of his opponents to the bill. He didn't talk about the big need; rather, he itemized the impact on individual single cities.

The parallel is that parents and staff care more about their school (local) than the district (national) as a whole. This is a strategy often used in winning support for building projects, such as listing what upgrades each school will get if a bond passes, but it can be applied to a much wider range of resource shifts.

As a superintendent, I was determined to add fourteen reading teachers in the district. This was a global view and not overly compelling. At a budget forum, the president of a school PTO pushed back, saying the paras in her school were wonderful, and they didn't want to lose any of them. I was about to recite National Reading Panel and What Works Clearinghouse chapter and verse, but the principal of that school cut me off and responded: "Mary, we have 125 students who are not reading at grade level at our school. That's too many kids. What we are doing isn't working for most of our struggling readers. This budget will add 1.5 reading teachers to work with our kids and a half-time reading coach to work with our teachers. We need this. Our teachers want the added coaching because they're not happy with the results either."

Mary responded, "Oh, we would get more reading teachers and coaches . . . and our teachers want this?"

It was fascinating to watch the interaction. How many times did they say "we" and "our" in a one-minute exchange? Ten times. Had the parent and PTO president thought her school had no struggling readers? Did she think all these new staff would work everywhere but in her school? I assumed it was obvious that every school would benefit, but until the principal laid out the impact on Mary's school the effort seemed "a district" benefit, with a "local" loss. That all changed. Mary wanted these added staff, wanted to help 125 kids in her school, and wanted to deliver what her teachers needed. All politics is local, at least for Mary. After this meeting, we recast our message, giving each principal a cheat sheet itemizing the benefits on his or her school specifically.

Taken together, all of these messaging strategies try to find a balance between appealing to the head and the heart. Both are needed in equal doses. Sharing the numbers, explaining the reasons of why and why not, and being transparent all help build support from analytical thinkers. A clear vision and comprehensive plan that helps students will create an emotional bond with the budget, even one that includes some hard-on-staff decisions. One without the other is much less compelling.

8

GET THE MESSAGE
OUT TO ALL SUPPORTERS AND
POTENTIAL SUPPORTERS

*Consider New Strategies for Getting
Staff and the Public Engaged*

Communicating with the public (and staff) about the budget is very important, but no matter how many forums districts hold, no matter what time of day they offer them, and no matter how they publicize the forum, the audience is sparse and mostly the usual suspects plus those negatively impacted. The unpleasant ritual typically begins with a PowerPoint presentation by the superintendent, followed by speaker after speaker criticizing each cut and shift in resources. The aftermath is often a skittish school board who heard much pushback and stakeholders who don't feel heard. The alternative seems worse: little communication, bad press, and added pushback for engaging the public on important decisions.

Transparency, stakeholder engagement, and public input are the holy trinity of budget communications from the perspective of most school boards. While critically important, these communication approaches can seem like a case of damned if you do, and doubly damned if you don't. The well-worn ritual of soliciting public input on the district budget can feel like a Hobson's choice with no good alternatives, a task to get through rather than a lever for change.

Being armed with thoughtful messages and bold, comprehensive plans worth communicating leads to the final challenge of passing smarter budgets: how to get the word out in a way that builds support for student-centered budgets that include some pain and disappointment. It's hard, but a number of approaches can increase the odds that district communication efforts will build public and staff support.

TALK TO THE UNDECIDED AND OPEN-MINDED

Even when you have a clear and compelling message, it's very time-consuming to mount an effective communication plan with the public and staff. Many district leaders, unintentionally, make it more time-consuming, harder, and less effective than it needs to be.

To understand why, it helps to think of staff and the community as fitting into one of four groups.

1. *Friends.* They almost always agree with your direction and plans.
2. *Undecided.* They are engaged and involved but haven't made up their minds either way.
3. *Adversaries.* Membership in this group can shift based on the topic, but they oppose the plan, often for good reason, such as their department is being downsized.
4. *Uninterested.* They feel K–12, school budgets, and town politics just aren't a high priority.

Too often, district leaders spend huge amounts of time debating their adversaries. This happens almost without conscious effort. Adversaries come to board meetings, flame on social media, and write letters to the editor. They proactively engage in the fight, and it's natural to respond. Unfortunately, most of them aren't going to change their stance. They won't (and perhaps shouldn't, given the pain to them and their group) support a smarter student-centered budget.

On the flip side, it's comforting and even uplifting to discuss, review, and explain the plan to friends. They provide very positive energy, but spending more time with them doesn't generate more support, since their support is already in hand.

It's best to concentrate communication efforts on the "engaged yet undecided" group. This may seem daunting because there are so many people in this group, they don't come to public forums, and districts seldom have a list with their names and contact information. Fortunately, the concept of "communication and influence nodes" can streamline reaching these critical potential supporters. It seems that in most districts—from suburban ones with two thousand students to urban ones with one hundred thousand students—a decidedly small yet influential group of people shape and voice public opinion. These could be parents active in PTOs, well-respected teachers, certain members of town boards, leaders of clubs or local organizations, elected officials (past and present), Little League coaches, and so on. These are often people who have titles or leadership roles (often unpaid or unofficial) and who, by virtue of their role and the personality traits that attracted them to it, talk to lots of people, shape public opinion, and have disproportionate sway in influencing others. This group is key to winning support for tough budget decisions because they can provide effective two-way communication with the undecided.

These influential, connected folks can help in many ways. Certainly, they carry much weight and can bring others along, but they also are important as honest critics. Do they understand your message? What concerns do they voice? Do they have a misunderstanding of key facts? What rumors have they heard? They can help shape your message, refine the plan to shave off rough edges, and pinpoint areas of confusion—winning support from this group helps improve communications with the public at large.

There is an emerging science of *influence mapping*. It is being used in rural Africa to determine who can be most effective in getting villagers to adopt healthier practices, in corporate America to facilitate effective teams after a merger, and in K–12 settings by savvy superintendents who have used it intuitively.

There are a number of concrete steps a district can take to help turn undecided yet open-minded fence sitters into strong supporters by tapping into a network of influential communication partners.

- *Make a list of names.* A good way to identify key influencers, both inside the district and within the community, is to map out who has influence.[1] It helps to get very specific about who these open-minded yet influential people are. Typically, it takes a large group to name the names. Some people may have insight into Little League coaches, but others will be more knowledgeable about the arts or town politics, or neighborhood groups.
- *Invite them in to the conversation.* Don't hope that they hear your message, but rather bring them together in small groups to hear directly from district leaders. It may be worthwhile to share your plans and message while it's still in development, thus identifying potential

challenges before final decisions are made. When as superintendent I had planned to raise athletic fees, we did just this. We learned from these opinion makers that it seemed unfair to charge all sports the same fee if the costs were different, and very unfair to exempt the arts from fees. Neither idea was on our radar screen, but both became part of the final proposal. In a sports-loving, fee-hating town, much higher athletic fees passed without too much pushback because we had learned from open-minded critics how to win over the public, and the key influencers were comfortable supporting the plan because they helped shape it.

- *Listen, don't sell.* When sharing your plans and message with key influencers, listen to their feedback. Jot down their questions, but don't try to convince them. It's easy to turn on the sales pitch and try to persuade them to support the plan as is. It's more important, however, to really hear all their concerns and misconceptions. Once you start rebutting their objections, they tend to become less candid, the opportunity to learn is lost, and their support diminishes.

- *Respond in writing.* Open-minded critics ask lots of questions. Why cut at the high school, but not middle school? Why math and not English? Much of the public will be wondering the same. It's a good practice to create a Frequently Asked Questions (FAQs) document and post it on the district website with your answers. It's important to organize the questions so the public can quickly scan for those relevant to them. Written answers also have the benefit of keeping the message consistent, since many of the influencers will be spreading the word and written answers can serve as a script for them.

- *Share the facts.* As a child, I hated when my mother answered my protest with "because I'm your mother, and I'm telling you to do it." Sometimes as a superintendent I found myself repeating this annoying habit. When I was questioned on a particular element of the budget, my inner monologue was, "Look, I have studied this for months and discussed it with my cabinet, we are the educational professionals, and we think it's the right thing to do for many reasons. Why don't you trust our judgment!?" A better answer would have been to share the facts that we used to come to this conclusion.

At its heart, the concept acknowledges two truths:

1. *People in an organization or community have trusted colleagues who are "go-to people" for specific needs.* Everyone in the King School goes to Mary for help with math lesson planning, many teachers go to Mark if they can't control the behavior of a student, Steve seems to always have the inside scoop on what the school board will support, and the Pop Warner coach knows what's going to help or harm the district's athletic teams.
2. *The go-to people are often unofficial leaders.* These influencers don't necessarily have any formal authority, and if they do, their status as a go-to person may be unrelated to their official role. The org chart isn't correlated to the influence map. In one district, the go-to math person was a teacher, not the director of math; the behavior expert was officially part of an autism program, but was the oracle for all things related to behavior; and the Title I director had the inside line to the school board's thinking on all topics, not just Title I.

There is now sophisticated software and a fast-developing art to visualizing influence in an organization, but there is also a down-and-dirty yet effective means of mapping influence in a school or district. Just ask a lot of teachers whom they seek advice from. As I was first launching a sweeping reading redesign effort, I informally asked every teacher I met for a month the following two questions:

1. If you had a student who was struggling to read, whom would you go to for advice, if you were unsure what to try next?
2. Whom would you recommend we ask to guide the district's efforts to help new teachers become more effective reading teachers?

The first question tends to identify trusted and influential teachers, and the second tends to identify respected administrators. The results were eye-opening. Every school had one or two go-to staff, and no one—absolutely no one—mentioned our director of reading. Interestingly, three principals did get named often as well as a few reading coaches in response to the second question.

My next step was to convene a focus group comprising these go-to people and seek their feedback on my soon-to-be-proposed reading reforms. They had great ideas, improved the plan, and with just a bit of prodding became the unofficial advocates for the sweeping shift in resources. Teachers and principals sought their opinion, automatically, since that's how they got selected in the first place, and they could give compelling answers because they knew the details of the plan and supported it.

The benefits of engaging key influencers are magnified because these trusted souls also typically have shared values with the colleagues and neighbors who seek them out. It's uncommon to trust someone if you don't respect their beliefs and values. This is a huge plus, given that most resource decisions have a significant value element and that there are conflicting values (student centered versus organizational stability). I have heard teachers, principals, or board members say, "I'm supporting this change because Mary is." They may not be fully convinced of the need or plan, but Mary wouldn't support a bad idea. Trust—not just logic, charts, or graphs—can carry the day.

Focusing on the undecided via key influencers is powerful, but as a cautionary note, adversaries can't be completely ignored either. Often, opponents to a shift in resources steal the stage, set the agenda, and frame the discussion. This is a motivated group. They are losing their jobs, or status, or something near and dear to them. They have a strong (and reasonable) desire to push back. Most often the benefit of any change in the budget is more diffuse, helping many a bit, while the pain often hits a few, but hard. As a result, adversaries are often active, loud, and persistent, following you to every forum and board meeting and jumping on social media with gusto.

It's important to calmly debunk their misinformation. Since "save our jobs" isn't the most compelling message, adversaries typically look for, or sincerely believe, a different set of facts and truths. In one district, for example, that was looking to reduce special education teachers and shift the funds to reading teachers and mental health counselors, the special ed staff proclaimed loudly, "The district's plan is illegal, we will be fined millions of dollars, and children won't get the services on their IEPs." Not true, but scary if it were.

This should lead to three FAQ entries:

1. Is the plan a violation of regulations?
2. Might the district be fined?
3. Will some children not receive services on their IEPs?

While clarifying misstatements is important, remember your audience isn't the upset people in front of you, but the engaged, undecided people who aren't in the room.

Listening, learning, and responding to the engaged but undecided group can help create support for difficult, student-centered budgets. Shifting time and effort from the in-your-face opponents or your strongest allies takes planning and discipline, but can yield widespread support.

WHO DOES THE TALKING?

Whether it's a meeting with key influencers, a briefing of the school board, or a public forum, the person who does the talking is as important as what is said. Too often, positional authority trumps ability to influence in determining who is at the podium. Influence mapping is helpful because it pinpoints people who can sway others. Underlying the rationale for relying on trusted colleagues rather than positional authority is the belief that facts alone aren't enough to win support. If the key to effective and persuasive communication were being able to convince people of a plan's merits, then a clear-minded, well-reasoned thinker with a bias toward data might be a great spokesperson. This nice, smart person could explain in simple English the "what" and the "why." Unfortunately, this person might be best suited for winning a high school debate, rather than winning the hearts and minds of key stakeholders.

Effective communication needs effective communicators—not a surprising idea. The surprise is *who* is an effective communicator, however. School systems have a formal hierarchy. Superintendents are in charge of principals, principals are in charge of teachers, and so on. Who talks tends to mirror this org chart–driven thinking. When presenting the budget or trying to gain support for shifts in spending, superintendents often do much of the talking. It's their plan, and as district leaders, it only seems logical that they present and explain. Sitting beside or near the superintendent during the presentation will be the central office department leaders. The central office folks are on hand to answer any detailed questions that may arise.

This org chart approach to selecting the key communicators isn't always effective in reducing pushback and winning support for tough budget decisions. The key shortcoming might not be evident to anyone in the room, and the presentation and discussion may feel like it went well. People listened and asked good questions, for which good answers were provided. Unfortunately, it's what happens next that's problematic. In the days that follow, teachers and parents start asking questions or sharing their opinions. When principals are queried, too often they distance themselves from the decision, with responses such as "The superintendent says we need to raise reading test scores, so he is cutting paraprofessionals. He never liked them much, doesn't appreciate what they do." This answer is not destined to win many supporters within the school.

View Principals as Key Influencers and Potential Public Spokespersons

Whether a superintendent plans on it or not, lots of people ask the principal about budget cuts, shifts, and new spending. Principals will talk to far more people than the superintendent and the cabinet. This can be very unhelpful. Keep in mind, most of the principals are good, caring leaders wanting to do what's best for kids. If principals aren't passionate supporters, the odds of winning over broad-based staff and community support diminish greatly. As it turns out, not only do lots of people seek the opinions of principals, but those opinions typically carry great weight. Parents, teachers, and school board members often consider principals a trusted source of unbiased information, and free from politics or the need to balance the budget. Superintendents may be at the top of the org chart, but they often don't have the greatest credibility. So why do some good school leaders undermine the district plans? A few reasons:

- *Because it's the district's plan.* If principals feel they were excluded from the decision making, they have limited ownership of the plan. It goes against human nature to defend a painful decision made by others. Principals often distance themselves from the decision because they were distant from the decision making.

- *Because they don't know the answers.* While the public presentation tends to focus on the big picture, such as "Reading is critical and our kids deserve highly skilled reading teachers," the morning-after questions are often very detailed, pragmatic ones: "Will Mary be supporting Johnny next year? Who will cover recess duty if the paras are gone?" The honest answer is "I don't know," which is not comforting. Sometimes a principal, feeling ill-prepared and unhappy that he can't answer these legitimate questions, might add, "They never think these things through. If we lose all the paras, it will be dangerous at recess."

- *Because they have doubts themselves.* Absent being part of robust joint fact finding, the principals may have the same concerns that teachers are sharing.
- *They misunderstand the plan.* This one surprises me, but it happens often in my experience. Even when principals have been part of the planning, some seem to walk away understanding the "what" but not the "why": "Yes, I know we are going to shift some dollars from paraprofessionals to add more reading teachers," and so on. They can and do share the details of what's planned. They stumble sometimes, however, in setting the context for *why* the change is being proposed, and the why is what will win over supporters.

Winning the active support of principals is key to winning active support from others, but district leaders must earn their support, not expect or demand it.

A simple step to help principals be more forceful communicators and advocates is to increase their level of certainty. Principals are trusted leaders, and they don't want to lose this hard-earned trust. As a result, I've seen some building leaders provide weak or vague answers when they aren't 100 percent sure. Yes, they were 99 percent sure that the superintendent said attrition would be used to reduce the number of paras so no one would be laid off, and yes, they were 95 percent sure that the Chief Academic Officer said the number of struggling readers was increasing each year, but they weren't 100 percent sure. So when asked why the layoffs, some principals will respond with a long, vague answer that dodges the question and raises anxiety in the questioner. Simply providing each principal with a fact sheet can turn a vague answer into a compelling one. Better yet, the principals can then share a copy of the fact sheet and help spread the truth. Some districts take this idea a few steps further. They provide talking points that map out the framing, set the context, and highlight key messaging. Principals appreciate these supports (if they believe in the changes), and staff and the public hear a more consistent message.

Taking the idea of the principal as key influencer another step further, in some districts principals are also the public spokespersons. After I had pushed through a few painful years of shifting resources, my political capital account was empty—overdrawn, actually.

Having fully engaged the principals in the planning and joint fact finding, I asked them to present many of the key shifts in resources to the school board and public. They also fielded the Q&A that followed. It helped a lot. They had more goodwill to draw upon than I did. The process also had an unanticipated benefit: it surfaced hidden fears or disagreements among the principals. Trying to not leave much to chance—and there is always a risk when you turn over the microphone to someone else—I asked the principals to rehearse the presentation and practice a mock Q&A session. I was surprised a few questions were answered "off script." It turned out that many thought the rollout was too fast, so they danced around any question related to timing. It was better to know this and address it head-on. With a modified, phased rollout they could support, their answers were strong, compelling, and energized.

First Share Trade-offs, Not Decisions

Regardless of who delivers the budget message, it helps to share the tough choices, not just the final recommendations. It seems logical that after months of research, hours of debates, and constant refinement, the proposed budget is ready to be shared with stakeholders in the schools and community.

Unfortunately, the audience hasn't spent months researching, debating, and wrestling with tough choices. They have spent just twenty minutes listening to hard decisions that don't sound like fun. The presenter hopes listeners will trust the judgment of the leadership team and realize these are the best decisions possible given much need, a theory of action, and limited resources. Often, however, the audience members pepper the presenter with questions, wonder why less painful alternatives weren't considered, and point out the downside of each shift or cut.

It's easy and natural for people to resist hard choices and to hope (or believe) that easier options must exist. Making stakeholders wrestle with trade-offs is a key element in building their support. This isn't the same as asking what they would cut instead; rather, forcing staff and the public to wrestle with trade-offs means, quite literally, giving them the real choices the district considered. For example, "If we raise class size by half a student, on average, this frees up $500,000," or "Raising athletic fees by $100 (subject to a family cap and sliding-scale payments) raises $300,000. These funds would support expanded middle school athletics and eight new reading teachers."

Having been through this process a few times, I have learned a few do's and don'ts.

Do:

- Include only options that the district would actually implement.
- Provide at least three levels of saying yes. This turns out to be very important. For example, ask, "Should we raise lunch fees by 10 cents, 25 cents, or 50 cents?" rather than just offering a singular option for, say, a 25-cent increase.

Stakeholders wrestle as much with the size of a change as they do with the change itself.

- Give choices that impact different levels (elementary, middle, and high school) and different areas (sports, arts, central office).
- Test the wording with focus groups first to be sure the options are easy to understand. Never underestimate how edu-jargon creeps into the conversation.

Don't:

- Link a specific cut or revenue to a specific new effort. This can be a bit counterintuitive. It seems logical that a rise in athletic fees could be used to expand middle school sports, but a dollar is a dollar and it can fund anything, such as drug and alcohol counselors. Keep the sources and uses of funds separate.
- Ask if you aren't planning to respect the results. It's reasonable to set a minimum required participation rate, but the risk to this process is that you are asking for input that's ignored at your peril.

Don't Ask If You Can't Deliver

Giving stakeholders a chance to weigh the alternatives is a novel yet controlled and productive way of soliciting public and staff input. Some of the more common approaches to engage with the public and staff, however, can be counterproductive and actually build roadblocks rather than clear the way for change.

The very common public forum falls short because few attend, and most in the audience are negatively impacted staff, their friends, and a small diehard group of regulars, but not the general public or average staff members. Public forums provide input from far less than 1 percent of the public, and nearly always highlight resistance. The dilemma this poses is that the forum asks for public input, but then leaders feel comfortable, perhaps, ignoring the input because it isn't actually representative. This further angers those who did come to speak and can make the involved but undecided think that no one wants the change and that the leaders aren't listening.

Technology has made it easier to reach larger groups of teachers and the public. Linking a survey to the district website, emailing SurveyMonkey surveys to parents and staff, and launching two-way text campaigns can connect the district to multitudes. Texting has become very effective for communicating with the public. Low-cost polling services like MindMixer allow the public to answer questions by text and share their ideas. The caution is that while the communication tools are new, human nature remains constant. Very thoughtful planning is still a must.

One district, determined to hear from the public in order to build grassroots support, utilized such a text-based communication service. At first the leadership was thrilled with the high level of participation. Thousands of regular people texted in their ideas for what they wanted more of and how they might shift resources. Joy turned to frustration a few months later. While the district valued the public input very seriously, the ideas offered included far more additions than subtractions, and many of the savings offered were against state regulations, wouldn't save much money, or conflicted with the district's theory of action. The district leaders used what they could and the text dialogue definitely shaped the proposed budget. It also alienated most of the participants!

Since the majority of the suggestions simply couldn't be followed, they weren't incorporated in the proposed budget and the public felt they were being ignored. The process created more pushback than buy-in. This isn't to suggest that either the idea or the tech tool should be avoided, but open-ended questions aren't likely to be helpful.

Perhaps these communication tools are best used in two ways. They can be very effective to understand values and framing. Asking what skills, traits, qualities, or knowledge stakeholders believe are important for our students can provide much insight into the outcomes the public values. This allows future budget messages to be framed around achieving these goals. If the community wants their children to compete successfully in a global world or to find happiness in a rewarding life, then weaving this into the message of why the district needs more reading teachers can connect budget actions to stakeholder desires.

The technology is also great for asking the public to choose between alternatives. Totally open-ended questions such as "What can be cut back?" or "What should we have more of?" can be replaced with specific choices and trade-offs.

A KINDER, GENTLER PUBLIC BUDGET FORUM

Technology is great, but the ritual of the public budget forum isn't likely to go away any time soon. A more focused public forum can be a good means of getting useful feedback while also building support for budgets that are tough but good for students. One large urban district seems to have perfected this approach. The new approach was born out of despair. The district sincerely wanted to hear from many stakeholders, but typically heard only from an angry vocal minority. The challenge seemed daunting. In a city of more than five hundred thousand people, most open forums drew one hundred regulars, mostly union officials and the politically connected. Attendees shared strong opinions, often swaying (scaring?) the school board, even though it's unlikely they represented the wishes of half a million people.

The district leaders tried a more controlled yet more representative process. Their first clever idea was to identify fifty diverse types of stakeholders and then map an existing organization or group to each of the stakeholder types. For example, the chamber of commerce could speak for local business, the IT Council for the growing tech community, the PTO for parents, the executive director of a public housing agency for transient students, and so on. They prepared a set of priorities and a rationale for why the priorities were selected. The document was just a few pages long, written in jargon-free language. On an invitation-only basis, small groups of these diverse stakeholder representatives came to hear the plan and give feedback. Multiple forums were held, so each group would have a "more than sound bite" chance to be heard. The questions were provided to participants in advance, such as "Which, if any, priorities are relevant to your constituents?" and "How could these elements be improved without increasing costs?"

Yes, these questions presupposed the plan wasn't open for wholesale change, and no, many who would like to have been heard (the regulars) weren't, but the reaction to the process was very favorable. Lots of people and groups had meaningful dialogue, which built understanding on both sides. Because only a small number of representatives were at each forum, they had substantive two-way dialogue, rather than the more typical three-minute speech followed by either a rebuttal or just another speech by the next in line for the microphone. They talked and learned. Equally importantly, they felt heard.

Avoid Jargon at All Costs

Regardless of the means used to communicate with the public, there are three rules that apply to almost any setting, document, or issue.

1. Don't use edu-speak jargon.
2. Don't use edu-speak jargon.
3. Never break the first two rules.

K–12 has its own language. It seems commonplace to those who live it, but bewildering to most of the rest of the world. It's so widely understood inside the walls of schools and central office that a few phrases can be shorthand for complex issues. Utter "unfunded mandate" or "supplement, not supplant" and educator heads nod, but eyes glaze over on Main Street.

Having watched hundreds of budget presentations, I'm confident that in more than half of them the public didn't really get the message because it was delivered in a foreign tongue. Such basics as where money comes from and where it goes can be hard for the average person to understand. One well-managed, thoughtful district accidentally ran into a buzz saw because the words spoken weren't understood. The superintendent tripped over central office jargon and never recovered. In an attempt to increase support, his budget plan included a seemingly popular decision to move control of some funds for the arts from the central office to each school. By shifting the dollars to the schools, principals could elect to offer band, jazz band, chorus, general music, or any combination of the arts. No school got a dollar more or a dollar less than the year before, but principals were empowered a bit.

This seemingly crowd-pleasing nod to site-based control, however, triggered a crisis of confidence. The superintendent announced the decision as "zeroing out band from the central office budget." He was technically correct in edu-speak. Since historically the central office made the decision about which schools offered band versus jazz or chorus, the funds for these positions were a line item in the central office budget even though all of the funded staff worked in the schools. The official line-item name was *band*, but it covered all of the arts. A band teacher in the audience stoked public ire via social media, posting that band was being eliminated! Angry parents, little kids with big tubas, and teachers angry upon learning of their impending layoff mounted a fierce counterattack. "Save band!" became a galvanizing cry against the entire new budget. Despite a few follow-on communications efforts, few people could comprehend how zeroing out band (at the central office) meant more options for students. In the end, the school board insisted band be restored, and virtually all of the other major resource shifts were also scrapped.

Edu-jargon can unintentionally cause lots of anxiety in other ways. One district announced sweeping cuts to Section 7 spending. Millions of dollars would be reduced to close the budget gap. At this point, I would like to ask the reader whether you would have supported deep cuts to the Section 7 spending. Not sure? Confused? Wondering what Section 7 is? So was everyone else! Section 7 was the seventh part of the budget document, which included a hodge-podge of programs managed by a wide range of central office departments. This part of the budget was so opaque that even few in the central office knew what was included. While every cut was carefully considered and a wise decision, presenting it as "Section 7 cuts" raised confusion and anxiety. Some felt it was an intentional effort to hide bad news rather than simply being inside baseball lingo.

Beyond the jargon of the sector, talking about budgets with the public and staff is hard, because many aspects of district budgets don't actually make sense to regular people. In what other setting could a leader say, in total honesty, that her budget is $50 million when she actually spends $65 million when all forms and sources of spending are counted? When the superintendent says "budget," she means operating budget. She often excludes federal grants, revolving funds, capital spending, and more. No one is telling a lie, but it can feel that way when the public gets an inkling that there's more money than the districts let on.

Talking about the operating budget, rather than total spending, can make the public think the district hides or plays fast and loose with staffing levels as well. When a superintendent says, "We are cutting 10 paraprofessionals out of 100," he means it. Why, then, if 120 people with the title *paraprofessional* actually work in the district, does he report having only 90 after the cut rather than the 110 who will return to work next year? Because the other 20 are "Title I paras," which are paid for by a grant and perhaps hired at the discretion of the principals. But, again, to the rest of the world 120 paras is 120, not 100, and confusion reigns.

Finally, few things are as confusing as talking about central office costs. The public generally dislikes spending money on the central office, preferring to have the dollars in the schools— for teachers, not administrators. Ironically, as referenced earlier, many districts greatly overstate how much is spent in the central office, underreporting what's actually spent on kids in schools.

Many staff members who work in more than one school (such as speech therapists), who are paid by grants (such as some special education teachers), or who are supervised by central office folks (such as instructional coaches) are listed as a central office expense. These staff members spend 100 percent of every work day in schools, and may never actually step through the doorway of the central office, yet they are often not listed as school spending but rather as central office.

These small confusions can be dismissed as semantics or "the way the state makes us budget," but they can greatly complicate talking to staff and the public and needlessly create pushback.

Build a District Budget That Speaks for Itself

An overlooked opportunity to communicate with the public about the budget is the budget document itself. Despite having a business background, earning an MBA, and having reviewed more than one hundred district budgets, I find most such documents incomprehensible. I can't distill the strategy or reason for new or old spending, it's hard to see any cuts, and it's very hard to know if higher spending in some places is driven by more staff, inflation, cost of living adjustment (COLA), or something else. In short, it's a lot of numbers without a storyline. Perhaps the most easily discerned facts from a typical budget are that a few line items went up by astronomical amounts, such as 400 percent or more, typically prompting a question about why there was such a large increase during tight times. Only on closer inspection does the questioner realize that occupational therapy travel rose from $50 to $200—yes, a fourfold increase, but only an extra $150 out of $50 million in spending.

The fact that many district budget documents run one-hundred-plus pages keeps most of the public from even trying to read them. This is a lost opportunity. Sure, the state or your accounting software may require one hundred pages of detail, but the public could have a shorter, more compelling version. Some districts produce budget documents for the public that run just a few pages, have more words than numbers, and clearly list district priorities and major spending shifts. These public-friendly documents explain what's important, summarize spending, highlight trends, and mostly communicate an honest, easy-to-understand story in paragraphs and simple charts, with just a page or two of numbers.

The private sector offers some powerful examples of effective budget communications. A quick glance through GE's annual report tells the reader how the company is doing, what it's been doing, and what lies ahead. It shares its financials in an easy-to-understand way and is an excellent communication tool. Even though GE is a Fortune 500 company with $140 billion budget, working in every corner of the globe, in a dozen disparate industries, the reader can, in about a minute, understand its budget, strategy, and results. In about thirty pages the document tells the company's whole story in much detail, but with more words and charts than line-item specifics.

To give you a sense of just how little a hundred-page budget can communicate, even many school committee members misunderstand their district's financial picture because their budgets don't tell a coherent story.

In one district, the school committee happily ended a contentious collective beginning negotiation by giving a generous increase in health benefits in exchange for a slightly smaller pay raise for the teachers. When the CFO pushed back, arguing that the final deal cost more than the raises originally requested by the union, a few board members were puzzled. These smart, experienced stewards of taxpayer dollars explained, "The district pays for the salaries, but we don't pay for health insurance. It's free to us!" They were half right. Nowhere in the hundred-page budget, which they reviewed carefully, questioned in great detail, and approved each year, was there a single dollar listed for health insurance. Unfortunately, this was an "off-budget" item that was charged to the schools through an accounting entry by the town comptroller. The district did in fact pay all of these health insurance costs, and the increased premiums led to teacher layoffs.

Many school budgets also do an awful job setting the context for the reader. It's often impossible to tell if enrollment is increasing or decreasing, if total staffing is rising or shrinking, or what programs or initiatives are being added or subtracted. They also seldom connect the story to past years. What's been the trend over the last few years?

Imagine a concerned citizen meeting a district leader in the grocery store checkout line and asking, "So how's the budget going to be next year?" The leader might say, "It's tough. Our enrollment is growing, but state funding to the schools was cut dramatically three years ago and hasn't recovered. We are adding more reading teachers, but to do so we have trimmed the number of administrators, reduced paraprofessionals, and raised athletic fees. It's a hard choice. But the new reading program has raised the number of proficient readers by 35 percent, so it's worth the pain!" In fewer than seventy words, the leader told a clear story. Even the most careful reading of a typical hundred-page budget that funded this plan wouldn't have revealed this storyline.

It's hard to underestimate how little many budgets communicate. In one district, big cuts in state aid had been offset by very large annual transfers from a reserve fund for three years in a row. When the reserve fund ran dry, the cuts that had been postponed finally came due. Unfortunately, almost no one, including many on the school board, fully realized that the district had propped up past budgets by draining its rainy day fund. Angrily, the board accused the superintendent of hiding past deficits, mismanaging district funds, and perhaps orchestrating a cover-up. None of this was true, but nor could anyone find such critical information in their one-hundred-fifty-plus-page budget. Lots of numbers, little information, and even less understanding.

PSYCHOGRAPHICS: SPEAK TO PEOPLE ABOUT WHAT THEY CARE ABOUT

As principals and the budget documents become storytellers, it's helpful to remember that not everyone in the audience has the same cares or perspective. In many districts today, it's common to think about customizing a message to different demographic groups in town. What will preschool parents think? How will high school parents react? What support can we garner from the business community, or families without kids in the school? It's great that districts think about connecting with unique groups differently, but this isn't the most effective way to customize the message. These groups lump together similar *demographics*—people with common attributes such as their children's ages—but within each of these groups there is still wide variation in how they will react to spending decisions. *Psychographics* is a more useful way to customize messages.

Psychographics is a fancy term for people's values, opinions, attitudes, and interests. It's a concept that is widely used in developing consumer marketing communication strategies. In many ways, it's a cousin to demographics, which describe a person's age, gender, race, and so on.

Traditional psychographic segmentation breaks the world into sixty-six groups, each with a catchy name. The White Picket Fence segment comprises families longing for a traditional, perhaps elusive, experience of dinners together, school plays, and children doing better than their parents.

The Bohemian Mix segment, on the other hand, comprises progressives who are dismissive of their parents' values and early adopters of new technology, contemporary art, and trends found on the Huffington Post. Interestingly, parents of preschoolers can easily fall in either category, and it's easy to see that different messages and even different communication mediums might resonate differently. The two groups are demographically identical but psychographically very different.

The White Picket Fence parents might be more influenced by the PTO president, want the Thanksgiving pageant, and read the local paper. The Bohemians are more likely to listen to their like-minded peers, get their news from Facebook, and want a multicultural art show for their children. To learn more about the sixty-six psychographic segments, search online for "Nielsen Prizm Segments" for a complete listing and descriptions.

I have seen a few districts intuitively use psychographic segmentation to help shape their communication strategies. One large district used something similar to the national segmentation scheme to deeply understand the values of its community members and how best to reach and impact them. The district came to understand the differing aspirations parents had for their children, from attending Ivy League colleges, to having promising careers in technical trades, to developing international awareness and multicultural appreciation. These values, not the age of their children, drove the crafting of plans and messages.

As a superintendent who at times struggled to connect with some stakeholders, I created my own K–12-centric psychographic profile of the community. Having gotten to know the town, and what issues seemed to energize different stakeholders, I found it relatively easy to build the segmentation plan. It included:

- *World Is Flat.* Highly educated, mostly new-to-town families who traveled much and worried about their children succeeding in a globally competitive world.
- *Local Pride.* Longtime, often multigeneration, residents who took great pride in our hockey, football, and other teams, and felt we had great schools and great teachers.
- *Bricks and Mortar.* Perhaps the most surprising group, they felt that the quality of our education was closely tied to the quality of our buildings, computers, and other tangibles.
- *Special Ed Moms and Dads.* As it sounds, they were very concerned about inclusion and meeting the needs of students with disabilities.
- *Not with My Money.* A very fiscally conservative, generally antitax group that believed the district wasted a lot of money and shouldn't get more.
- *The Invisibles.* Parents who seldom interacted with the schools. This included many new immigrants.

Armed with an understanding of the diverse community I wanted to communicate with, I tried to frame my message in a way that would resonate with each of them. To be sure, I didn't (and shouldn't) tell a different story to each group since this muddles the message, makes them feel like they are being pandered to, and ultimately undermines my credibility.

Additionally, people don't wear labels proclaiming their psychographic segmentation, so you don't often know who you are communicating with at any given moment. But understanding the key K–12 segments helped me craft a more compelling message.

My basic premise was that reading is critical, yet too many kids in the district struggled to read, so we needed to stop having paraprofessionals acting as reading teachers and hire more skilled actual reading teachers. We also needed to improve core reading instruction, and instructional coaches would help do just that. Personally, I was pleased with this logical story, as it was comprehensive and student-centered.

It didn't resonate, however. When I looked at it through the psychographic filter, it became clear why such solid educational priorities generated little excitement.

The World Is Flat parents viewed the effort as basic, remedial, and "so last century." Local Pride was insulted, deeply insulted, because it implied our schools weren't great (too many struggling readers) and our teachers aren't good teachers because they needed coaching. The Bricks and Mortar people saw nothing in it for them, the Special Ed Moms and Dads thought it was a big loss (fewer paraprofessionals), and the Not with My Money group were incensed that we wasted money on paras. The message didn't please anyone, even though it was good for kids and taxpayers alike. It resonated with my principals and central office because they were a different K–12 psychographic segment: Bread and Butter Ed Reformers. We had, unknowingly, crafted a message that appealed to us: adopt and expand proven best practices, with gusto and scale.

Without changing a single element of the plan, we changed the framing and messaging. We didn't lead with the National Reading Panel best practice research or our mediocre reading scores. Instead, we talked about the rising complexity of what kids read in middle school and high school, and we explained that higher-order thinking skills are built upon a solid foundation of comprehension and fluency. The World Is Flat parents started to see elementary reading as a gateway to the more exciting twenty-first-century skills they valued. Ironically, we had known this and believed it, but had focused on the more basic skills when we originally talked about the plan. We also shut up about our past shortcomings, and focused on the changing demographics in the district. We cited more special ed, more ELL, more mobility to explain the need for coaching—bad teaching wasn't the driver, but rather a new reality calling for new approaches. We also stressed that teachers wanted this help. Local Pride wasn't so insulted anymore.

The plan always included a hyperfocus on pairing students with special needs with these new skilled reading teachers and using software as part of the intervention model. Highlighting these elements won support from the Special Ed Moms and Dads and Bricks and Mortar group. In the end, the proposed reading initiative became a very popular, well-supported effort. Almost everyone saw the proposal's value in terms of what they valued. It was the same plan, but with a much more compelling message.

Every district will have a different mix of psychographic segments, and many leaders will have intuitively thought about what resonates with their community, but getting specific and identifying those features by name can help bring structure to crafting compelling messages.

It's also valuable to think about the different internal staff segments and what they value. Too often I fell into the trap of thinking, "Principals support X" or "Teachers will oppose Y." The truth is seldom so cut and dried. I had principals who felt kinship with Local Pride, and others with the World Is Flat. Some constituted the Bread and Butter Ed Reform group, while some teachers seemed to be in two other segments entirely: Data Is a Four-Letter Word, and We're Professionals. The first segment had a visceral negative reaction to state tests, and framing the message as "we're helping kids struggling to read" was much less upsetting than saying, "students are not proficient," even though they were the same kids. The second segment wanted respect for their skills and training, and they appreciated the concept that struggling readers needed the most skilled teachers to help them.

After all the hard work of crafting bold and comprehensive budgets designed to help the most students as much as possible with limited resources, an effective communication strategy can push the proposed budget over the finish line.

REASON TO BE OPTIMISTIC

Tight budgets, rising student needs, higher standards, political pushback, and competing interests are hardly the ingredients for a story with a happy ending. Or are they? I suspect many of you who started reading this book did so because you were worried about how to make ends meet or how to hold on to the teachers and services you have. You were thinking it was a survival guide for budget battles.

I hope by the end of the book, you're feeling more optimistic. As I have worked with and observed skillful leaders and cultures that have grown more comfortable with change, I have come to be very optimistic about our chances to raise student achievement notwithstanding tight resources and all the headaches that addition by subtraction brings.

My optimism comes from two directions. The first is that *despite* tight resources districts can fund the new programs, services, and staffing they need. The second is that *because* resources are tight districts will be more likely to fund more effective programs, services, and staffing.

This first reason for an upbeat attitude should be no surprise. Eight chapters detailed strategies for shifting funds and winning support for smart, student-centric budgets. Real districts, with unions, parents, veteran teachers, and siloed administrators, have overcome all the usual reasons to resist tough budget decisions and have successfully put these strategies to work.

Just recently I was working with a group of district leaders facing a terrible and all-too-familiar situation. Funding was declining, salaries and benefits were increasing, and the budget gap for next year was staggering. This followed a bruising budget battle the prior year, a battle that seemed to be all casualties with no winners.

As the district leaders entered the room to tackle next year's budget, they had little energy and less joy. After I welcomed them and thanked them for coming, one veteran administrator said, "Don't thank me. I'm only here because I have to be. I would rather be any other place but here. I have been through thirteen budgets, all bad, and this will be worse. We have an impossible job."

While he was more vocal than most, many others in the room shared his sentiments. They felt they needed many millions to raise achievement, and rather than getting these dollars, they would be cutting, and cutting across the board like they always did. Over the next few months the district embraced a strategy of shifting funds, repurposing staff already in the budget, and engaging in some joint fact finding. More importantly, they realized the need for a short list of priorities, all driven by a common theory of action.

While this story hasn't reached its conclusion, so far there are more smiles than frowns. The team feels that they can craft a bold and comprehensive plan to raise achievement and that they have the strategies to win support for the needed changes. Interestingly, the administrator who would rather be anywhere else shared that he was optimistic that a path forward was possible, maybe even likely. If a bruised and frustrated administrator is now optimistic, so am I.

While no one would ever wish a tight budget on anyone, there can be a silver lining to all this difficulty. I have seen many districts stop ineffective programs and even embrace very structured program evaluations to identify what's working and what's not. Sure, they were motivated to learn what works because they cared about students, but they hadn't actually ever done formal evaluations until the dollars got really tight. They no longer could afford to continue programs that didn't work, and when those programs were ended two good things happened. First, students didn't receive ineffective supports, programing, or services anymore. Second, new, better options were provided in their place.

Lastly, as detailed throughout the book, building support for making tough budget decisions requires agreeing to a common theory of action, engaging in joint fact finding to really know the truth, conducting program evaluation to learn what works, engaging and enlisting principals, building comprehensive plans and sticking with them, and effectively communicating with stakeholders both inside the district and across the community. These "good for the budget" strategies, fortunately, are the very same ones that can help raise achievement, even if money were free flowing. It seems that doing right for the budget can build the capacities and practices that serve many other worthwhile efforts as well, and that's the best reason to be optimistic.

NOTES

CHAPTER 1

1. http://educationnext.org/the-middle-school-plunge/

CHAPTER 3

1. Lauren Weber and Elizabeth Dwoskin, "As Personality Tests Multiply, Employers Are Split," *Wall Street Journal*, September 30, 2014.
2. Lyle Kirtman, *Leadership and Teams: The Missing Piece of the Educational Reform Puzzle* (New York: Pearson, 2013).
3. http://jpschools.org/about-us/district-school-performance/

CHAPTER 8

1. Douglas B. Reeves, "Of Hubs, Bridges, and Networks," *Educational Leadership* 63, no. 8 (2006), 32–37, http://www.ascd.org/publications /educational-leadership/may06/vol63/num08/Of-Hubs,-Bridges,-and -Networks.aspx.

ABOUT THE AUTHOR

Nathan Levenson is currently president of the District Management Council. He began his career in the private sector, starting as a strategic planning management consultant, as the owner of a midsized manufacturer of highly engineered machinery, and as a turnaround consultant helping struggling firms. A passion for public education led to a career switch, which included six years as a school board member, as assistant superintendent for curriculum and instruction in Harvard, Massachusetts, and as superintendent of the Arlington (Massachusetts) Public Schools.

Nathan was hired as superintendent to be a change agent in Arlington during a turbulent time in a divided community. He helped create and champion an intensive reading program, which reduced the number of students reading below grade level by 52 percent, and revamped special education services, leading to a 24 percent improvement in academic achievement in English and math. The Rennie Center for Education Research and Policy identified Arlington High as a best-practice school for reducing the special education achievement gap by more than nearly all other schools in the state (a 66 percent reduction).

Putting the phrase "It takes a village to raise a child" in action, the Arlington Public Schools built partnerships with local nonprofits to provide—at little or no cost—psychology counselors, social workers, family counselors, a diversion program, drug and alcohol counselors, and a community-wide coalition to help keep students safe from substance abuse and stress.

As president of the District Management Council, Nathan assists school districts across the country in raising achievement at lower costs. His work in special education and resource use is on the leading edge of thinking and practice.

He has published research for the American Enterprise Institute, the Fordham Foundation, the Bill and Melinda Gates Foundation, and the Center for American Progress. He has also been an advisor to the US Department of Education and state departments of education, and is a national speaker on the topic of doing more with less.

Nathan received a BA from Dartmouth College and an MBA with distinction from Harvard Business School, and is a graduate of the Broad Foundation Urban Superintendents Academy.

INDEX